How to Use Politicians to
Get What You Want

How to Use Politicians to Get What You Want

Scott Colvin

First published in Great Britain in 2011 by
Biteback Publishing Ltd
Westminster Tower
3 Albert Embankment
London
SE1 7SP

ISBN 978-1-84954-086-5

10 9 8 7 6 5 4 3 2 1

A CIP catalogue record for this book is available from the British Library.

Set in Sabon LT Std
Printed and bound in Great Britain by
Thomson Litho, East Kilbride, Scotland

To my late mother Brenda

Contents

Acknowledgements   xi
Foreword *Sir Stephen Sherbourne* CBE   xiii
Introduction   1

Chapter 1: Politicians

The expenses saga   7
What makes an MP tick?   12
Are we too hard on them?   19
The surprising power of an MP   26
The 'Penning' effect   28
Why MPs attack corporates   30
How an MP's office works   32
How to contact your MP   36
How NOT to contact your MP   43
MEPs and councillors   48
The new relationship   53

Chapter 2: Corporates

What's the problem?   58
Why consumers get frustrated   60
The loss of faith in big business   64
Why do companies lose touch?   67
What makes a CEO tick?   71
The fear of sudden events   74
Consumer watchdogs   78
The fear of politicians   82

The role of regulators 83
How to contact a CEO 87

Chapter 3: Lobbying

What is lobbying? 91
A brief history of lobbying 94
Professional lobbying 99
Where next for lobbying? 101
How to lobby 103
Case study: The Gurkhas and Joanna Lumley 105
David vs Goliath 108

Chapter 4: Campaigning as an individual

Don't get mad, get even 111
How to make a complaint 113
The power of blogging 119
Why do complaints fail? 120
The minister for consumer affairs 123
The pressure point 124
Case study: The gas boiler 127
Case study: The Gatwick Express 133
Case study: The pizza 136
Case study: The clamper 139
Case study: The wine company 142
Case study: The house builder 144
Conclusion 147

Chapter 5: Campaigning in your community

What is your campaign? 149
The general rules of community campaigns 151
Construct a message grid 152
Setting the right tone 154
Top down and bottom up 156
Set goals and objectives 156
Understand your audiences 157
Get out the vote 160
Assess your own team 161

Opportunities and threats 161
Developing a campaign strategy 162
Message themes 162
Media plan 163
Why 'local' matters 164
Case study: Save our hospital 166
Case study: The post office 169
Case study: The mobile phone mast 174
Conclusion 177

Chapter 6: The nuts and bolts of the modern campaign

Fundraising 179
Global campaigns 182
Facebook campaigns 183
Twitter campaigns 184
Doing radio 185
Doing TV 185
Public speaking 186
Local newspapers 188
Localism 189

Conclusion

Lean into it 193
The last word... 195

Resources 199

Author biography 203

Acknowledgements

This book could not have been written without the love and understanding of my wife Hannah, and my children Oliver and Kerr. Thanks to Wray for keeping the troops fed and watered so I could cross the finish line.

Thanks also to Iain Dale, Shane Greer and the rest of the Biteback team for having faith in my idea, and to Kevin Bell and David Canzini for showing me how politics really works.

Foreword

Here is the paradox: people, confronted by government heavy-handedness in their day-to-day life, are desperately looking for help. Meanwhile, Members of Parliament are genuinely committed to help yet the gap between politicians and the public has never been wider. The expenses scandal has tarred all MPs with the same brush. Politicians seem to talk their own language. So, not surprisingly, people ask themselves, why bother to participate?

Scott Colvin provides the answer. He has worked for and with politicians. He knows what makes them tick. He knows what works. And he has a track record of fighting campaigns and mobilising political support in order to get decisions changed.

Having also worked within the corporate sector, he understands what buttons consumers should press to make things happen.

In this book, Scott draws on his own experience – not only as a political operator and as a company executive but also as an individual consumer and citizen – to show how people power really can work and achieve results. He is insightful, entertaining but above all instructive. This book shines a light on how government and companies operate behind closed doors. It will also serve as a practical manual on how to overcome political and corporate bureaucracy.

It is a positive book. It demonstrates that where there's a will, there's a way. And Scott shows us the way.

Sir Stephen Sherbourne CBE, former political secretary to Prime Minister Margaret Thatcher

Introduction

This is a book for people who do not want to enter the political system, but simply want the system to work better for them, for their family and for their community. Most people do not wish to spend any more time with their politicians than they have to. It is not a lack of understanding, or apathy. It is not the dumbing down of Britain. It is the widespread belief that politicians are not making our lives better and have grown ever more detached from the daily challenges that we all face in the real world.

I am driven by the belief that anyone can learn the techniques needed to win campaigns, both for themselves and for the greater good of the area in which they live. Acquiring these skills does not require you to have pots of money or even lots of time to spare. It does not require you to tell lies, cheat, use violence or have impressive qualifications. It does not require an understanding of David Cameron's concept of the Big Society. You simply need the tools to understand how the political process works, how the corporate world works, and then you learn the particular techniques which will make both audiences more likely to do what you want.

As you take your first tentative steps into this brave new world, actually making politicians 'do what you want' may seem beyond you. Most of us would not dream of approaching a politician unless it was the very last resort, but they do still retain a surprising level of power. It is easy for a professional lobbyist who plies his trade in the hustle and bustle of Westminster politics to claim it is easy, but what about the majority of people whose only participation in politics is to vote in a general election? This book demonstrates that you can influence politicians in a positive way by understanding what makes them tick. You should not be fearful, afraid or intimidated by the process of lobbying. After all, you elect politicians, and therefore you have every right to be better represented by them on the things that matter to you.

In the first chapter I will consider the role of politicians and how it has changed, and continues to change, in the light of the expenses scandal which has so fundamentally damaged our political system. In chapter 2 I take a similar look at the state of the corporate world, especially the role of the chief executive, and provide insights into what drives their thinking and behaviour. For those new to the concept of lobbying, I provide a short introduction in chapter 3 to what it is, where it has been, where it is likely to be going and how its techniques can be used to empower everyday people to begin to reclaim some of their consumer rights. Finally in chapters 4, 5 and 6 I look in depth at how to start beating the system, using the same methods politicians and corporates have used against you for years.

Politics is driven by the three Ps: personalities, power and pressure. Personalities shape the political discourse more than ideologies, because it is the jealousies, commitment, egotism, genius and stupidity of our politicians that defines who wins and who loses. That is ultimately why I am so endlessly fascinated by what takes place in the corridors of power, but also why most people are turned off by it. They see the bickering, the childish tantrums and the one-upmanship and they bury their heads in their hands. They wish politicians could work on issues that are actually important to the majority of us, but the reason why that will never happen is because of our second 'p': power.

The insatiable desire to achieve and attain power is at the

core of politics. At its most noble, this desire manifests itself as a determination to end poverty, educate our children and keep the streets safe from crime. But at its most basic, this desire is simply a means to an end; to win for the sake of winning.

Lastly, politicians live their professional lives handling lots of pressures, from their local party associations, their constit uents, the whips, and the media. The right type of pressure, exerted in the right way, and at the right time, can change the way that people in politics behave.

There will no doubt be criticisms of a book which urges you to involve your MP in your day-to-day battles as a consumer and in your community. Surely national politicians, some will say, should be left alone to represent us on the big stuff – the economy, defence, the NHS and schools. But this misses the fundamental point that we no longer believe that politicians are making our world a better place. In fact, for many people the opposite is true. Whether it is Britain's engagement in the war in Iraq or the tatty state of our local streets, we feel let down by the people who represent us. Unsurprisingly, the attitude of deference and respect no longer exists, replaced by either dislike or apathy. Over the past few decades, MPs have seen their influence on the major global issues rescind, forced instead to cut ribbons, kiss babies and hand out prizes at the church fête.

But despite the provocative title of this book, my criticisms of politicians are balanced by a sympathetic view of the enormous pressures they face each and every day. Being an MP is tougher today than it has ever been, and they are being asked to do more for less. However, if we can find a way to harness their influence and powers, we can win personal and community battles we did not believe were achievable. In short, everybody wins.

In the course of this book, you will note that I am less sympathetic about the corporate world. I never fail to be amazed at just how out of touch and unresponsive some of our biggest and most successful companies have become. For example, there is nothing at all wrong with private firms trimming their costs by outsourcing some functions overseas, but a huge barrier between brand and customer has been erected with call centres being moved out of the UK. The bureaucracy has increased but the customer service has diminished. Close your eyes and think about your nearest major town. Whereas it once featured a mix of big name retailers and local shopkeepers, I bet it is now dominated by the former. Most of us could guess the exact layout of any shopping centre in Britain, which is perhaps why we are always so pleasantly surprised when we go abroad and see the local baker, fishmonger and grocer still competing with the supermarket chains. But we only have ourselves to blame because we have allowed companies to let standards slip. With a shrug of the shoulders and a murmur of resignation, we have convinced ourselves that companies have become too big to care. But like politicians, we can hold them to account, and force profound change in the corporate culture in the process.

This book requires you to spend some time thinking about the way you are treated as a consumer. It needs you to look around your community, and at the politics you see on your television and read about in the newspaper. If you are happy with your lot in life and how you are represented then close the book now and put it back on the shelf. But if you are not content with it, and wish for change, then it is time that you got up off your backside and did something about it.

This means taking on the companies which treat you badly. Refuse to accept the mismanagement of your local area, and ask your politicians to help you with the issues which to other people will be trivial, but mean the world to you. Get a refund from your credit card company, get better customer service from your water provider, and work with other local parents to open a new school or band together to save the

Accident & Emergency facility in your town. This amount of effort and engagement no doubt sounds a daunting prospect, but hopefully an exciting one too.

Chapter 1: Politicians

The expenses saga

An MP climbs into a taxi at Victoria train station for the short journey up the road to the Houses of Parliament in June 2009. He is visibly shaken and distressed. As cabbies often do, the driver asks if his passenger is OK. The MP says that many of his colleagues have been accused of expenses fiddling by the *Telegraph* and he fears his own reputation could be sullied in a future story. 'It's so unfair. We work our socks off for scant credit and little money. And now we are all being tarred with the same brush as only being out to line our own pockets,' says the MP, now close to tears. The cabbie looks on with some sympathy, 'Don't worry mate, you're obviously one of the good guys.' As the taxi pulls up outside Parliament, the MP pays him, nods his thanks and gets out. As the taxi pulls away the MP suddenly runs after it, waving his arms frantically. The cabbie stops and rolls down his window. 'Sorry,' says the MP, 'I forgot to ask for a receipt.'

OK, so I made this up but the fact that it feels true neatly sums up the sense that MPs failed to grasp why the public was so angered by what they did in regards to the claiming of expenses.

For a brief time, years before the controversy broke, I had toyed with the idea of standing for Parliament, egged on by a couple of friendly MPs. It was initially an attractive idea, but there were a considerable number of hurdles the idea had to clear. Although the biggest of them was the potential impact on my family, given that the hours and lifestyle are so unsociable, one of the other concerns was the potential financial sacrifice. I was reassured, however, that although a career in Parliament was unlikely to make me rich, it could still provide more than enough income through help with mortgage payments, food costs and even furniture. It sounded odd at the time, but like many people outside of Parliament, I cannot claim to have fully grasped the extent of the 'wink wink' culture that would come to haunt MPs just a few years later.

The MPs' expenses scandal slowly built over a number of years, beginning in 2005 when Freedom of Information (FOI) requests were separately made by two journalists and an FOI campaigner, using the newly available powers brought in by Tony Blair's government in 2000. In the beginning, it seemed a rather niche issue, interesting for Westminster watchers and political junkies, but not really relevant to those outside the system. The general public, it is fair to say, did not really understand how the system of payments made to MPs worked. It could be argued that many MPs didn't understand it either.

The House of Commons authorities tend to move slowly and they did not disappoint when faced with this emerging crisis. The Palace of Westminster is a dazzling place of history and tradition, but it also remains out of touch despite the promises of radical modernisation. Its strange rules and procedures offer no hope of comprehension to the casual observer, and the expenses system was therefore just a symptom of a wider problem of an institution which had become too inwardly focused. Rather than offer most of what the campaigners wanted, they blocked everything they could, using every available excuse and legal obstacle. The problem is that the more they resisted, the more curious the public and media became about what they had to hide. A Westminster issue was about to go global. It was not just the authorities who tried to resist the calls for full disclosure, as MPs from all parties fought hard to prevent the release of information.

Although the eventual release of the expenses information was always going to be explosive, it could have been managed so much better by ensuring that it was given context, rather than waiting for the information to be leaked to a major national newspaper which ruthlessly, but understandably, maximised its impact.

When the full information was released by the *Daily Telegraph*, it was akin to a paving slab being lifted in the garden and finding lots of nasties underneath. It was staggering, even to people who work in and around Westminster, to believe how many MPs, some very senior, had committed such outlandish acts of greed. Given that MPs have always been closely scrutinised by the outside world, it is a surprise that so many of them had simply deluded themselves into thinking that something which was permitted was therefore also ethical. Even if it could be argued that their behaviour was loosely within the rules, it is remarkable that they chose not to imagine what the general public would say if their expense claims suddenly came to light. They did not believe the campaigners would ever succeed.

Another own goal was that by delaying the release of information for so long, MPs and peers had ensured the worst possible time for the data to be made public, namely during one of the biggest global economic downturns in history. As people in Britain experienced pay freezes at best and job losses at worst, news that parliamentarians had been feathering their own nests for years was never going to make them popular.

On 8 May 2009 the information began to be released, starting with members of the then Labour Cabinet, followed by junior ministers and significant backbenchers from the same party. But before the Left could cry foul, the *Telegraph* duly turned its focus on the Conservatives, starting with the shadow Cabinet before moving on to its backbenchers. The Liberal Democrats were the last to receive the *Telegraph* treatment but were helped by the low numbers of representatives in Parliament. Even though they were not immune from the scandal, they had just sixty-two MPs compared with Labour's 356, and the Conservatives' 198.

Had the *Telegraph* not published the information, it would have prevented much of the information about the so-called 'flipping' of homes from being released. This practice was arguably the most controversial of all the revelations, as it was revealed that MPs and members of the House of Lords were able to ensure they could nominate which of their properties were their primary and secondary homes in order to maximise the expenses they could claim. An MP could tell the Commons that as their second home, they wanted some of its renovations, fixtures and fittings to be paid for by taxpayers. Once the renovations were complete, the MP could then redefine it as their primary residence, meaning their other property could then be refurbished.

In one infamous example, the former Labour MP for Luton South, Margaret Moran, was found to have nominated her secondary residence as a property in Southampton, a two-hour drive from both her constituency and her place of work in Westminster. Even more scandalous, Moran had claimed £22,500 to solve a dry-rot problem in her seaside abode just days after nominating it to the Commons authorities.

What made the release of the expenses data so compelling was that it effectively meant it was being conducted in 'real-time' with *Telegraph* journalists scouring the data day and night, ready to figure out the stories for the next day's copy. Most, if not all, MPs and peers went home each evening wondering whether they would be next, as they saw their colleagues and opponents fall one by one. Each day brought more and more shocking revelations, everything from MPs claiming for help with mortgages which had already been paid off, to the really petty, such as claims for Remembrance Day wreaths, duck houses and moat cleaning. Interestingly, it tended to be the petty expenses which caught the public's eye rather than the outright alleged fraud. Getting caught re-nominating one's second home was at least ballsy and offered a significant financial benefit to the MP, whereas claims for a single packet of Maltesers, a tin of dog food and a one pence mobile phone call just looked squalid.

Publicly, various party leaders have talked tough, with several MPs and Peers dragged through the courts, and Parliament has introduced strict new rules which should prevent future abuses. Yet in private, few MPs (at least, those who were MPs before the last general election) accept that they did a great deal wrong. It is not unusual to hear the following lines from politicians: 'We simply followed the rules', 'We didn't break the law', 'There were a few bad apples, but we've all been tarred with the same brush', 'We thought we had a system of allowances, not expenses.' In truth, they were encouraged by their whips and Commons officials to claim as much as they could to top up a salary which had been held down by successive governments wary of public disapproval.

This potted history does not answer the key question, namely why so many MPs messed up so spectacularly? They are currently paid a salary of £65,738 per annum, which is a small figure for someone who joins Parliament from a profession such as law, medicine or from a plum job in the City. However, for someone who was elected having been a teacher, nurse, or a trade union representative (a considerable number from the Labour Party were elected from these types of public sector roles in 1997) the salary remains very good indeed, perhaps more than double what they previously earned, especially since there is always another candidate (either from the same or a different party) who is willing to replace them.

Debate has raged for many years about whether MPs are paid too much or not nearly enough, but the demand for places in the House of Commons has always been much greater than the capacity, so it is difficult to maintain the argument that the best people are put off from a career in Parliament due to low pay. The oft made threats that recent events will make it even harder to persuade good people to come through the system seem to be baloney. The intake from the 2010 general election is certainly not inferior to those who arrived in 2005, and is probably better given that it is a more representative mix of skills and people. We will get to the reasons why politicians choose this type of career later in this chapter, but needless to say the vast majority of MPs are not motivated purely by money. They are primarily driven by restless ambition, albeit combined with a desire to perform public service.

What makes an MP tick?

If you were to ask random strangers on the street what they think about MPs, how many would say something positive? Even people who participate by voting at each and every election tend to take a dim view of the political class.

In my own qualitative research, I was able to distil the comments into five categories, and the responses that people gave were:

› *Distant* – MPs are rarely visible locally or nationally unless they hold a senior position in government or opposition. However, they always seem to appear when it suits them, namely around election time.

› *Greedy* – Even since the clampdown on MPs' expenses, they are seen to be greedy, happily telling people to tighten their belts and putting the squeeze on hard-working families. Yet they award themselves pay rises, enjoy gold-plated pensions and even have subsidised restaurants and bars in the House of Parliament.

› *Pointless* – Arguably the worst accusation of all, that the role of an MP serves no purpose. The average back-bencher has no influence with senior decision-makers even in their own party. They are forced to subjugate their real policy views, being told what to do by their own party managers if they ever hope to progress their careers. In the constituency, they try to avoid controversy wherever possible, simply a face in the local paper cutting the ribbon at the church fête or holding a shovel at the planting of a tree.

› *Untrustworthy* – This is partly linked to greed, but it is actually a much wider problem. MPs make and break promises with ease, using clever spin and slippery explanations when taken to task for doing so. They also radically shift and change ideological positions in a way which does not seem normal to most people. One minute Michael Portillo is the right-wing hard man declaring 'who dares wins' at the 1995 Conservative party conference; the next he is promoting gay rights and the decriminalisation of cannabis. Few people in the real world change their outlook so radically and easily.

› *Out of touch* – Whilst accepting that the role of an MP is important, some people simply see politicians as being out of step with the everyday struggles of folk in Britain. Two of the three party leaders all went to exclusive private schools and all went on to either Oxford or Cambridge. They are all wealthy in their own rights, and have lived most of their working lives amongst the chattering classes of West and North London. They do not know what it feels like to fear a rise in interest rates or worry about the quality of the local state schools.

Decision-making at a very senior political level has changed radically over the past few decades. Gone are the days of meaningful debates around the Cabinet table, replaced instead by the 'sofa government' of trusted, unelected advisers. Tony Blair positively revelled in it, Brown continued it and Cameron is making its membership even more exclusive. This means that there are more disenfranchised politicians stalking the corridors of Parliament than ever before, many feeling powerless, yet not able to come to terms with their lack of influence.

However, many politicians still retain an extraordinary level of self-regard and often lose sight of an honest assessment of their abilities. Getting elected is such a tough business, both being adopted as a candidate by the local party, and then winning the right to represent the constituency in question. This quite often engenders a feeling that they must be special to have endured and survived such an ordeal. For many people entering Parliament for the first time, it is thrilling and exciting to suddenly have a job which guarantees them some level of importance. The local and regional newspaper will usually give them a weekly column to muse on the issues of the day, their face will often appear on television and their voice on radio (at least locally), people write to them and ask their views on a whole range of subjects, and lobbying firms invite them to lots of parties and receptions. If the MP then gets to join a parliamentary select committee (cross-party groups of MPs who shadow the activities of each government department), they have powers to order any UK citizen or government minister to appear before them and answer questions.

The newly-elected former bank manager of a local branch in a small town could suddenly get the opportunity to grill the governor of the Bank of England, or the Chancellor of the Exchequer. The best part is that the senior executive or minister is unlikely to put up too much of a struggle, as being rude might mean a damning report – with all the subsequent bad publicity that comes with it – or even being hauled in before the committee for a second time. So with that in mind, it is understandable that some MPs allow their role to go to their heads, and occasionally lose touch with reality. The next election is always presumed to be four of five years away so some put off the hard graft in the community in favour of enjoying the fruits of their labour by fully living the Westminster life.

One of the major drivers of getting selected as a candidate

locally was the likelihood that he or she was perceived to have the potential to achieve high office. The panel would not have cared whether the candidate had been to the constituency before his selection and neither would the electorate given that MPs tended to be older types who had already made their money outside of politics. It was accepted.

Today, however, the story is very different indeed, and a candidate who cannot demonstrate some reasonable link to the area they are attempting to represent is unlikely to get very far. Candidates will look closely at the list of seats likely to come up before a general election and trawl their family history for some evidence that an aunt might have lived there, or a second cousin might have worked there. Given how geographically small the United Kingdom is, it remains a mystery to me why it should matter so much, but it does.

The reason it matters to the local party, and why it matters to the electorate, differs. For the former, they know that either lacking local links or refusing to physically move house to the constituency can be a significant factor in the final outcome, especially if fighting the Liberal Democrats who redefined 'localism' in an electoral context. Take Anne Milton MP, who has represented the Surrey town of Guildford since 2005. She was selected as the Conservative candidate in 2002, at a time when she was living with her family in Reigate. The distance between the two towns is approximately fifteen miles and given that her children were settled in school and they enjoyed their family home, they planned to stay put until nearer the likely date of the next election. If she won, she would immediately move to the constituency. In any sane world, this would be perfectly acceptable. But politics is not often sane and her Liberal Democrat opponent, the sitting MP Sue Doughty, started sending out leaflets heavily criticising Milton for not being local. The inference was that she did not care about the constituency. Given the majority for the seat was so small (just 538 at the time), Milton had to respond by incurring the huge expense and disruption of moving house just to prevent it becoming a political issue.

For the electorate, the issue with being local is a desire for that representative to understand the individual nuances of the town or part of a city. Being local means you probably went to the local school, and have family still living in the area, so you have more invested besides the job of being MP.

Being Prime Minister, or reaching one of the other major offices of state, requires great skill and public standing. After all, there have only been fifty-two male and one female prime ministers since the first in the early eighteenth century. Churchill, Thatcher and Blair all had a certain 'X Factor' which appealed to voters at election time. The level of self-belief amongst politicians tends to be higher than in most other professions. One forlorn MP once told me that the only difference between him and David Cameron was that the latter had been promoted by his friends in the media. There was no acceptance that the current Prime Minister is more mentally agile, media savvy, or just plain talented, but simply that he had picked the winning ticket in a political lottery. Examples of such self-delusion do not usually exist to the same degree in the corporate world where a middle-ranking manager is usually honest enough to accept that the chief executive or chairman of the company has skills they are unlikely to possess or ever acquire. Most of us might convince ourselves that we deserve to be paid more money or be given a better job title, but not that we are capable of addressing an AGM with 1,000 angry shareholders in attendance, or overseeing a major redundancy programme.

But this self-delusion is important if you are going to get to know your politicians a little better. They are all chasing a dream that one day they will get the opportunity to pull the levers of power; not just by voting in the House of Commons with the other hundreds of representatives, but as part of the behind-the-scenes team. To the credit of the vast majority of MPs, they would use this power in a constructive way, pursuing public policy changes for (what they perceive to be) the greater good.

The first Green Party MP, Caroline Lucas, would no doubt choose to focus on imposing measures to cut carbon emissions, as that is her passion. For the Tory right it might be reform of the benefits system or cutting taxes. For the Labour left it might be the imposition of windfall taxes on energy companies or fines for bankers. I am generalising, but you get the point.

The good news is that we live in a democracy. The bad news is that this means politicians are entirely dependent on your vote at election time to hold office, leading to the depressing fact that every elected politician in this country (and beyond) tends to consider every major decision on the basis of its electoral consequences. This does not mean that they are solely interested in your vote, as the motivation of public service remains strong, but if they do not obsess about staying in power, then someone else will beat them.

History is littered with politicians who have succeeded in their chosen political or policy aims but were then ejected at the next possible occasion. Take our most famous Prime Minister of all time, Winston Churchill. Internationally recognised as the man who organised Britain into a fit shape to take on the might of Nazi Germany, he was voted out of office at the next general election in one of the biggest landslides of the twentieth century. It was not because he was unpopular, just that his skills in war were no longer seen to be relevant for the job in peacetime.

So despite being one of the aspects of politics that creates cynicism amongst voters, it is unfortunately unavoidable. Put simply, you cannot get elected without asking people to vote for you, but it is this very act which plays to the preconceived view that politicians only care about one thing. Local politicians, whether they be councillors or your MP, come and knock on your door with a passionate interest in your community coincidentally just around the time when an election looms.

They will ask you whether there are any local issues which you care about. You might tell them that the streetlight at the end of the road has been broken for six months. They promise to get it fixed (and sometimes they actually do) but not before checking which party you are planning to vote for. There is little benefit getting thanks from a life-long Labour voter if you are a Conservative candidate, which is why parties use a list of known voters when they canvass in the run up to polling day. They mark where someone does not support them, and there is a good chance that they will not deliver a single leaflet to them or knock on their door ever again.

That said most voters do not mind being canvassed as long as the politician has kept in contact with them throughout the rest of the year, keeping them updated on what they are doing in the ward/constituency. If a local politician is especially effective, they often end up attracting supporters of other parties anyway, as most people are less loyal voters in local elections. This is one of the ways in which the Liberal Democrats managed to build a strong foothold in local government.

Politics has become professionalised over the past couple of decades into a genuine and immediate career option for someone studying at university. This is why an increasing number of party hacks make the next step into standing for a seat. A route often pursued today is to study politics at university, then after graduation head to Westminster to work as a researcher to an MP. These jobs are very lowly paid (and some, 'internships', do not pay at all) but they do offer a fantastic opportunity for graduates who suddenly find themselves in the midst of very senior politicians within the grandeur of Parliament. This role allows them to learn how politics really works – not the theory taught to them by professors in their student days, but in the bruising and unforgiving modern political world, where fortunes can change quickly. After working for an MP for a while the researcher might try his or her luck with their chosen political party's headquarters, especially if election time is less than a year away. The alternatives are to become a lobbyist or join a think-tank or pressure group. Either way, a lot of the individuals involved begin looking for a seat as early as their mid-20s. So far, they have nothing more than a university degree in politics, followed by three or four years working in Westminster. This lack of experience does make it difficult to see how they can make suitably informed and wise decisions.

This marks a significant change from the past when it tended to be predominantly men in their mid-40s upwards who entered politics once they had made enough money in their chosen profession. The one advantage of this system was the experience that the individuals had gained in the 'real world', which usually allowed them to make better informed choices about the impacts of any given new policy measure. They also tended to arrive at Parliament with little training in the communications techniques that all MPs now seem to adopt, which meant for a more honest debate and led to real characters being on the green benches. But perhaps my spectacles are rose-tinted.

Are we too hard on them?

For most MPs, getting elected to the House of Commons will have been a tough and expensive business. Even the brightest candidates can find it extremely difficult to get the ultimate prize for any aspiring parliamentarian: a 'safe seat' (i.e. a constituency which has such an unassailable majority that one party can be certain of victory).

One current Conservative MP I know applied to over fifty constituencies before he finally found a seat in which to stand. He estimates that it cost him nearly £60,000 of his own money to be a candidate in terms of paying for campaigning activities and the inevitable loss of earnings.

As a fledgling MP they will also soon discover that the party they represent expects total loyalty, especially in key votes. The performance of every MP is closely monitored by the whips, and reported back to the Chief Whip who wields enormous influence. Any sign of dissent could cost them future advancement, often meaning that they have to support policies they don't actually agree with.

To most sane observers, the role of an MP is utterly dreadful, not least because you have so many people to please. The average seat has around 70,000 constituents, but they also need to juggle the party's local association members, parliamentary colleagues, the whips, and various special interests and lobby groups. Of course, there are millions of people in this country who do mundane jobs to make ends meet and struggle on the minimum wage, but it remains true that anybody who seeks a balanced, family-oriented life would be risking it all to become an MP.

We British love to complain, but we moan about MPs without considering what they do, and what their role is. You no doubt presume they sit around ordering from the John Lewis catalogue, planning the next long lunch and visit to a West End massage parlour. That is certainly the impression offered by much of the recent media coverage of their roles in the wake of the expenses revelations. In reality, some MPs can get up to 200 emails a day, along with piles of mail and endless telephone messages. They will also be asked to take part in media interviews, photo opportunities, meetings of the parliamentary party, welcome groups of schoolchildren, and still find time to vote when the whips tell them to. Here is what constitutes a typical day for an MP, provided by someone elected in May 2010:

06.00	Wake up and help prepare breakfast for the children
07.00 – 08.30	Clear the previous day's emails and update website
09.00 – 10.15	Attend local economic development conference
10.30 – 11.30	Open local community health centre

11.30 – 14.00	Return to conference to chair Q&A session
14.00 – 15.00	Travel to House of Commons
15.00 – 15.30	Meet with local UK Borders Agency staff, who are trade union members
15.30 – 18.00	Work with parliamentary staff to review and respond to constituency casework
18.00 – 19.00	Attend meeting of the backbench committee to discuss parliamentary boundary review
19.00 – 20.00	Attend meeting of an All Party Parliamentary Group (APPG) re: Parliamentary Voting System & Constituencies Bill
20.00 – 22.00	Brief pause for dinner, then listen to debate on Fixed Term Parliaments Bill
22.00 – 22.30	Attend voting
22.30	Leave House of Commons, arriving home at approx. 23.30

Even the cruellest heart would find it difficult to disagree that this is a gruelling schedule, especially given that this is just for a humble backbench MP. A government minister's workload is even tougher, with considerably greater levels of scrutiny. Yes, Parliament still has its fair share of oddballs and no-goods, but it also has a great deal of talent, with some very interesting and bright people elected in May 2010.

Job security is practically non-existent, given that a general election can be called at almost any moment, but at the very least within five years of the previous one. An MP who finally realises their dream of getting elected to Parliament can be, just a few years later, unemployed, tainted as a one-term failure and subsequently humiliated in the jobs market. The days of a retired or defeated backbench MP snaring a highly paid directorship are largely over, with few companies willing to take the public relations risk of taking on a politician with baggage, which many will have.

In many cases, being an ex-MP probably makes it more difficult to find a new role in the future, unless they have a very specific qualified profession such as law or medicine. Therefore they are taking a considerable risk by entering Parliament in the first place, as 'safe' seats are increasingly rare. A recent example was the humiliation of the colourful Liberal Democrat MP Lembit Öpik, arguably best known for dating a Transylvanian pop star and an ITV weather girl.

Lembit had a very large profile both locally in his seat of Montgomeryshire and nationally, had worked his parliamentary seat assiduously for thirteen years and arrived at the election count on 6 May 2010 with the bookies offering unpromising odds of 25–1 on him losing. Yet that night his career came to an end when the teller revealed that he had lost to the unknown Conservative candidate Glyn Davies on a swing of 13.2 per cent. Had you stayed awake for that part of election night you would have seen Lembit, stumbling from his humbling defeat, subjected to a live grilling by BBC hard man Jeremy Paxman. Even his worst enemies must surely have felt some measure of sympathy for him, but you might assume that once the interview ended, so did his ordeal.

Unfortunately for him, and the other defeated MPs from across the parties, the vanquished are not treated with a great deal of dignity and respect in the process of leaving the House of Commons. They are given just a week to pack up their possessions and shred every last piece of constituency correspondence, some accrued over twenty years or more. They are sometimes literally shoved out of the office which they have resided in for so long, their support staff made redundant, and the doors locked.

Some former MPs do perfectly well once they leave Parliament. High profile figures such as Michael Howard or John Prescott have been elevated to the House of Lords where they will remain for the rest of their lives. No election is required, just the patronage of their respective party leaders is needed to immediately return them to a legislative role. Others attain plum roles as non-executive directors, paid handsomely for a day or two a week to advise the boards of major UK or foreign companies.

If your local MP is young and recently elected, then the pressure upon them to keep all audiences happy is especially high. An old stager such as Ken Clarke will barely care what people think about him, after so many decades at the forefront of decision-making. If he had to leave politics tomorrow, he could happily return to his corporate roles, and retire a rich man. But a career politician in their late twenties or early thirties is constantly looking down the barrel of a gun, just one false step away from unemployment with no clear idea what to do with their peculiar CV. When Gordon Brown was facing a potential coup from within his own Cabinet, one of the key figures was James Purnell, who resigned in the hope that it would trigger the Prime Minister's downfall before the 2010 general election. Unfortunately for him, Brown survived and Purnell quit Parliament just months later. A year on from being touted as a future Labour leader and Prime Minister, his promising political career was, at least temporarily, over at the tender age of forty.

Some defeated politicians are forced into the only career option available to them, trading their knowledge of Parliament in return for a job at a lobbying firm. A good example of this is Andrew MacKay, one of the high profile Conservative victims of the expenses scandal. Without getting into the nitty-gritty of his case, MacKay had everything going for him prior to May 2009. As David Cameron's 'eyes and ears', he acted as parliamentary gatekeeper to the man who was to become Prime Minister just a year later. Everybody treated MacKay with great respect, from his Conservative colleagues hoping to be promoted, to companies who wanted to better understand where Cameron stood on a given policy issue.

When he fell from grace, it was a very public humiliation, with Cameron left with no choice but to cut his man free. What complicated matters further was that his wife, former journalist and MP for Bromsgrove Julie Kirkbride, was also implicated in the controversy over the use of second home allowances. After an even more ferocious and unseemly battle, she was also forced to announce she would stand down (although she was subsequently cleared of the expenses charges). This meant that a political couple, both well connected within different wings of the party, suddenly saw their lives irrevocably changed, with neither being an MP. Both MacKay and Kirkbride subsequently became political consultants, advising private companies on how the new government operates. Decent jobs but hardly comparable with being one of the Prime Minister's key fixers based in and around 10 Downing Street, as MacKay would have been.

Even worse for current MPs who might be defeated at the next election, the so-called 'parachute payments' they used to receive have also been changed. This money was paid to former MPs to help them to readjust to normal life and to give them time to find a new job; it was worth tens of thousands of pounds, depending on length of service. However, at a time when so many people up and down the country were being made redundant without the benefit of this soft-landing, sympathy amongst the British public remained in short supply. An official review into parliamentary expenses recommended the payments be abolished, which would increase the pressure to win even more so.

But before we get too carried away revelling in the misery of MPs, we do need to accept some responsibility for how the modern politician behaves. The obsession with 'spin' comes about because we hammer politicians who say something interesting and different. If an MP criticises immigration levels, they are branded racist; if they question levels of tax for the middle-classes, they are branded selfish and ignorant of those in poverty. We may not choose to agree with the views that we hear on our news channels and in the newspapers, but to force people into resigning on the basis of expressing an honest opinion is surely absurd.

This demand for politicians to resign for being caught

saying or doing something we do not agree with feeds into the way political parties then begin to behave. The Blair administration copped a great deal of grief for making communications such a central function of its time in government, but it had only done so because previous Labour leaders such as Michael Foot and Neil Kinnock had been so ruthlessly denigrated by the media.

On the one hand, poll after poll suggests that the British public want honesty and individualism in Parliament yet are the first to support a sacking if someone steps out of line. This has led to the emergence of a new breed of politicians who are young and untainted by scandal, but ultimately bland. When choosing candidates in a range of seats at the last general election, all three parties often plumped for management consultants, former special advisers and policy wonks with no real experience in industry, manufacturing, or running small businesses. Many made the jump straight from party HQ to Parliament. It is understandable why so many such candidates were chosen. Many were absolutely flawless in terms of their personal records and conduct, which left their opponents with little ammunition. But do we really want 650 MPs who are unable to do or say anything colourful or edgy? At any political party conference it is always the speakers with something to say who draw the crowds – Ken Clarke, Peter Mandelson, Alastair Campbell, and Michael Portillo – rather than the pristine and self-controlled MPs of today. There are still a few stars in the Commons who have become well-known, at least within Westminster, for great skills of political communication but these examples are becoming rarer. We get the politicians we deserve.

Very few prime ministers since the war have overseen changes which were recognised as radical at the time. The post-war Labour government, with the creation of the National Health Service was clearly game changing, as was Thatcher's privatisation programme and right to buy scheme in the 1980s. But otherwise, the instinct of modern governments is to sustain power before all else. Even Tony Blair has admitted that his first four years as Prime Minister were not used effectively, saving his most radical plans until after his resounding victory in 2001. Chasing headlines and opinion polls is an especially depressing fact of modern political life.

The surprising power of an MP

One of the weaknesses we attribute to MPs is their perceived lack of real influence over the issues that matter to us. Will they agree to cut a ribbon at the local nursing home? No problem. Do they have the power to keep the town's A&E service open? Unlikely. Despite this, you would be surprised by just how powerful an MP can be in the right circumstances. MPs are the forgotten consumer support and as a source of help, they should not be underestimated.

Needless to say, even the most humble backbencher will get a meeting with a CEO of most companies in the FTSE-100 if they pursue it. In my dealings with major corporates, I cannot think of a single example where an MP failed to get a meeting with a chief executive. For example, I doubt many MPs who have sought a meeting with the likes of Sir Terry Leahy, the phenomenally successful leader of Tesco, have been turned down, despite the huge demands upon his time.

A parliamentarian related to me that she had requested a meeting with the chief executive of her local water company, having received a number of letters of complaint from her constituents. To her surprise, her request was initially turned down and she was instead offered a meeting with a middle-ranking customer services manager. Given that letters about the company continued to pour in (excuse the pun), the MP would not take no for an answer and went directly to the CEO's office, where a face-to-face meeting was finally agreed. For reasons I will explain in the next chapter, this reluctance of a CEO to meet a politician is extremely rare, and this particular corporate leader will have done himself little good in being so obstinate. Not only did he offend the local MP and sour their relationship before it had even begun, but he was still forced to go through with the meeting he had tried to avoid.

The power of an MP is that, as long as they refuse to give up, they can get directly in contact with any major business leader, council chief executive, headmaster, or government official they wish to. The chief executive of the water company, having failed to dodge the meeting, could do very little once the MP persisted. He had all but admitted that he could not be bothered to find a short amount of time to meet with the representative of an area, which was packed with 70,000 of his customers, given that water companies enjoy local monopolies. If the MP was motivated to do so, she could have raised parliamentary questions about the company, written a stinging opinion piece in the local newspaper about the company's lack of respect towards its customers, and generally made the CEO's life very difficult.

Broadly speaking, companies see MPs in two categories. Firstly, people they want to see because they are decision-makers, and secondly those they have to see to avoid causing offence. The former group have a powerful hold over the company in question because they can have a direct impact on the 'bottom line', whilst the latter are not proactively chased for meetings unless a specific issue arises.

MPs have evolved as their powers have been gradually stripped and eroded by a long era of 'sofa government', where a few close political friends dictate the policy agenda. Back-benchers have had to adopt lobbying techniques in order to get anywhere with the issues that matter to them. New MPs are given tips by the older guard about the variety of obscure parliamentary procedures which can be used, and it is always interesting to see which of the new intake learns the ropes more quickly than others.

MPs can also make companies and public sector bodies jump. They can be an irritant. They can ask lots of questions in Parliament, including to the Prime Minister, and initiate short debates in the chamber. They can table an Early Day Motion (EDM), a mostly pointless activity but it could directly name a company or individual, and the media is always happy to make an EDM sound important when it suits the story. They can write a column in the local newspaper, or simply submit a press release. They can even try to introduce a new piece of legislation via a Private Member's Bill, and although barely any have ever made it into law, the real purpose is to create publicity for the issue in question. If the MP is a member of a select committee they can call on the chairman to initiate an inquiry into a particular company or sector. In fact, select committees have the formal power to compel witnesses to attend, specifically to send for 'persons, papers and records'. They have a great deal of access to decision-makers, which is not always welcomed by the minister in question, but is an inevitable result of being together in the voting corridor on a regular basis, or in the Commons tearoom. Just a quiet word here or there knocking the conduct of a company could influence the way it is perceived by the minister.

Politicians increasingly like to be on the side of what they consider to be good or right, and companies are finding it ever more difficult to influence policymakers directly. The days of long, boozy lunches in smoke-filled rooms between politicians and corporate interests are thankfully long gone, which means that every campaigner has a chance to be heard. In the case of a consumer dispute with your credit card company, a politician today is much more likely to be on your side rather than that of the multinational bank. In a community campaign, well-organised local residents can be more attractive to an opposition party than the company they are protesting against, even if that company is important to the economic well-being of the country.

The 'Penning' effect

In the general election of 2005, Conservative MP Mike Penning became the representative of the Essex constituency of Hemel Hempstead. He won with one of the smallest majorities in the country, narrowly beating Labour. With such a tiny win, Penning knew he was going to have to work his seat solidly in order to retain it a few years later. It is likely that he would have held on anyway, as he is a hard-working MP. But less than a year into his tenure, a major oil storage facility, Buncefield, exploded.

The damage to the area around the site was horrendous and the fire burned relentlessly for several days. The so-called rolling news channels (i.e. BBC News 24 and Sky News) had the story running all day long for a whole week. In order to fill that amount of air time with interesting developments, and given that there had been damage to property but mercifully not to people, the town needed a spokesman. Not only was Mike a former firefighter but he was also a former journalist, and he made the most of both skills.

He became the voice of the town in the following days, talking to radio, television stations, foreign media, and most importantly doing the rounds in the community to hear people's stories and be their middleman in discussions with the authorities. Anyone watching the news at the time would have wondered when Penning managed to get any sleep.

This episode sealed his reputation, and by the time of the next general election Penning stormed home with the biggest Labour to Conservative parliamentary swing in the entire country, a staggering 14.5 per cent. He had taken a close marginal seat to a safe one in just five years. He was also rewarded with a government position at the department for transport, and is likely to remain on the frontbench for a number of years.

Penning would probably admit that he does not have the policy or presentational skills of some of his fellow ministers. But what he demonstrated at the time of the Buncefield explosion was a ferocious work ethic, combined with a genuine desire to bring together the community which had been so shocked by the events that had befallen the town. He demonstrated the benefits both to his own career and to the local community of being actively engaged with his constituents. Politicians will need to evolve in similar ways to Mike Penning if they are going to stay elected.

Why MPs attack corporates

Politicians like to flex their muscles outside of Parliament, and beating up the odd corporate leader or major brand can win them kudos with the media and certain pressure groups. It demonstrates that they are outside of the grubby sphere of influence so often believed to exist between politicians and business. This is clearly easier to do in opposition, as being in government means you tend to want to talk up the economy, whereas the team on the other side of the despatch box has no such restrictions. Those MPs who flex their muscles are not restricted to the heavyweights on the frontbenches either, as even the lowliest of MPs can decide to take on Microsoft, GlaxoSmithKline or McDonalds, and get a fair hearing.

The Liberal Democrat MP Norman Baker is an example of a politician who has made an entire career out of being an irritant to the corporate world, using his parliamentary position to challenge and question the activities of many of the big brands in the FTSE. Not to doubt his sincerity in the issues which he raises, but he has also used it to his personal advantage by positioning himself as the plucky challenger of conventional thinking. In his constituency of Lewes in East Sussex he has built a huge majority in a seat which used to vote Conservative without a second thought. In many ways he has been the embodiment of the ideal local MP, with a high profile in the town, a high profile nationally, and a general sense of action and momentum. This is combined with a reputation for being outspoken and not fitting neatly into the party system.

Even Prime Minister David Cameron started his bid to become the leader of the nation by attacking the corporate world. Having seen polling data which demonstrated that voters associated the Conservative Party with big business, Cameron and his team decided to rebut and challenge this stereotype by being counter-intuitive on a whole set of public policy issues, saying and doing the opposite of what people expected Conservatives to say. He set about creating a number of high-profile public attacks on companies who he believed were not behaving in the right way. He publicly criticised the high street retailer WH Smith for offering half price chocolate bars with every purchase made in the store. The company clearly believed it was giving its customers what they wanted, and argued that they were simply offering responsible adults a range of products. But Cameron had spied a way to highlight the growing obesity problem in this country in a cunning way. In a speech on emerging health threats, Cameron slammed the company for its unethical practices. The issue became so difficult for WH Smith that it was forced to provide fruit at every counter too, to offer an alternative to chocoholics. Even today, the fruit remains in store – but so does the cut-price chocolate.

Buoyed by the success of this first foray into the corporate world as party leader, Cameron then moved on to criticise the clothing retailer BHS for selling what he perceived to be inappropriate items of clothing for young children, such as padded bras and 'sexy' underwear for 10-year-olds. Once again, it worked a treat as the tabloid outcry in support of the new Tory leader's words led to the items being withdrawn from sale. Many years later the owner of that same clothing chain, Philip Green, was appointed by David Cameron as an adviser to his government. Political intervention clearly directly influences the way businesses operate, and vice versa.

It has to be said that MPs do attack corporates for the wrong reasons too. Often they attack a company in ignorance of the facts, having listened to only one side of the debate, or having been seduced by conspiracy theories spouted by a pressure group. Or they simply see an opportunity for self-promotion arise and go for it, even if they do not especially care about the issue in question. There are MPs famed for being critics of big pharmaceutical companies, energy providers, and bankers but very rarely do they appear to have made an effort to hear the other side of the story. The problem is that an MP cannot be an expert on every single sector, so they therefore rely on media coverage for their information. That is why it is refreshing to see an MP who considers each issue on its merits rather than slavishly following public opinion or the advice of the whips.

Many MPs on the centre left of British politics see it as their job specifically to scrutinise the behaviour of the private sector, just as the right tend to get more hung up on apparent abuses in the public sector. A sizeable number of Labour MPs have had an involvement in the trade unions movement before entering Parliament, so they bring with them an attitude which treats corporates with suspicion. But do not think that simply because an MP is left-wing or right-wing, he or she is always going to side with a trade union or corporation. In fact many Conservative MPs are scathing about big business, whilst some Labour MPs have distanced themselves from the unions.

How an MP's office works

Although you might have a vision in your mind of an MP living in luxury, surrounded by a vast team of advisers, spin doctors, media managers and tea makers, it is only senior Cabinet ministers who have anything like that level of support. The rest are assigned cramped office space conveniently located but in a pokey part of the Palace of Westminster. An MP who I worked for had access to more than one office, but by far the worst was in Norman Shaw North (Westminster building) where the office was shared with two others, one of whom was a member of a rival party. The office had barely any natural light, was dusty and smelly, and it was not unusual to arrive in the morning to be greeted by a dead rat on the carpet or on the desk.

The most opulent offices available to MPs are usually those in Portcullis House, but that is only because they are clean rather than spacious. At one time Portcullis House was the most expensively built office space in the UK, with 250 offices costing around £235 million to construct. But with its limited space and wood panelling you would think you had walked into a store cupboard, rather than the office space for a representative of around 70,000 people.

Inevitably, each MP arranges their office staff in a different way, but the typical set-up is to have a PA to manage the diary, with a research assistant on hand to keep the MP up to speed on the progress of legislation or produce background briefing for a committee hearing. Alongside this core team is sometimes a dedicated caseworker, i.e. someone who is there to follow up specific constituency issues. This person might be based in Westminster, but just as often they will be working from the constituency, as MPs increasingly put a higher value on having knowledgeable support in their local office.

When you write to or call your MP, you will almost always get through to someone immediately who is able to handle your query, which is at least an improvement on the experiences most of us have when dealing with large companies. There are a very small handful of MPs who even answer their own telephones if they are in the office, but this is certainly the exception rather than the rule.

Every MP's office is busy, and the emails, letters and telephone calls flow regularly throughout the day but, if you have not contacted an MP before, you are likely to be surprised at how easy it is to get your request or grumble in front of them.

Having once worked in an MP's office, my abiding memory is of the huge filing cabinet groaning with letters from constituents. My MP had only been in Parliament for eight years yet some individuals had written over 500 letters to him, and a dedicated drawer in the filing cabinet had to be made available for just such people. The types of letters we received ranged from the sublime to the absurd. There were some genuinely moving cases of people who had lost their jobs, were being denied access to their children, or were writing from prison. One correspondent had seen a member of their family die in a car accident and was campaigning for safety improvements to a local road.

One person also wrote to claim that he had evidence that the then Prime Minister Tony Blair had given MI5 permission to spy on him, through the ingenious use of invisible helicopters. Although the correspondent got a fulsome and polite response, I took a gamble and decided that the story was probably not true and there was therefore no need to alert the spooks. If you spend enough time processing constituents' letters, you begin to realise that the key to identifying disturbed people is the erratic nature of their handwriting.

The amount of correspondence received by MPs often becomes the yardstick by which they measure the importance of any given issue to the community they represent. That is because they know that few people take the time to put pen to paper or fingers to a keyboard. Those constituents who write hundreds of letters are considered repeat offenders, and the repetition of their various moans and groans will tend to work against them. What makes an MP sit up and take notice is when he or she starts getting letters from a range of people on a given issue; the more specific the issue, the greater the attention from the MP.

If a number of letters are received about the ongoing war in Afghanistan, it is unlikely to garner any great reaction from the MP, simply because a backbencher cannot single-handedly halt a conflict spearheaded by our only remaining superpower. However, if the letters are about the introduction of parking charges on the seafront, then the MP will know a direct threat to his majority has swept into view. The total number of letters does not even have to be that great, as more than five letters on any given issue will often make its mark. The rationale is that if this many people have separately taken the time to find the MP's email or postal address and commit their thoughts to paper it probably means that at least another 100 care passionately about the issue. Those 100 people are likely to have families, friends and colleagues in the constituency, and ultimately this means that real votes may be at stake.

Although MPs always have to contend with being hampered by their own party's actions in government, such as a war or the handling of the economy, the deadly issue they need to look out for is the controversial local one. For all the anger directed towards an MP who votes in Parliament for a controversial policy, nothing matches the anger felt when a hospital or post office closes. Incidentally, this is why some MPs privately do not like their own party ruling on the local authority, as decisions made in the council chamber can damage the MP too. All it takes is a town hall decision to increase the councillors' allowance, or the closure of the local library, and the MP gets tarred with the same brush. Does the MP stay loyal to his or her colleagues on the council, or decide to swim to safety before the ship sinks? My hometown frequently changes hands at a council level from Conservative to Liberal Democrat, and back again. This means that single issues could decide the fate of the ruling party, which keeps them alert to new and emerging local issues and ensures that every vote is fought for.

This will hopefully encourage you to believe that writing to your MP is not a waste of time, especially if you can find others in your community who feel equally passionately. Letters or formal emails are difficult to dismiss. When a letter is sent, it arrives with the MP's secretary who will briefly read through the text and place it into a suitable pile, ready for the next time the MP comes to the office. If the issue requires further study, the researcher in the office will seek information from either their own web search, or from the House of Commons Library.

When the MP comes to the office, he or she will be given an update on the most important issues constituents have written about. When a specific issue is mentioned a number of times, the MP knows it needs to be closely monitored. If the issue is new to them, they will ask for the team to follow it up so they can adopt a position in the future. On a very local level, checking with the local councillors or local constituency office would be the easiest way. If an issue is related to party policy it becomes more complicated, as usually the MP has no choice but to ask for a standard line to take from the party's HQ. That can sometimes be frustrating for the MP, especially when the position they hold is at odds with the national policy.

Anything complicated will be discussed and the MP will offer an opinion as to a way forward. The rest will be quite simple and a letter quickly prepared and signed.

How to contact your MP

Apologies in advance for stating the bleeding obvious, but before you start any campaign you need to identify who your local representatives are. This information can be gathered via the internet (a list of resources can be found in the 'Resources' section at the end of this book). In most instances, your list of representatives will consist of a Member of Parliament, a number of representatives for your region in the European Parliament, plus up to three local authority councillors. Please note that this slightly differs in areas where some powers have been devolved (i.e. taken away from the UK Parliament) such as Scotland, Wales, Northern Ireland and London which have parliamentary/assembly members too.

Make a note of the relevant names, their political persuasion and write down any contact details which may be listed. If you are feeling especially keen, you may want to find out further information about them, especially your MP. Although it is not always totally accurate, Wikipedia is a good place to begin as it will offer you a quick pen profile of the MP in question. It is not essential to source this information, but you might find some interesting details which are relevant to your future campaign, as well as a photograph. For example, if you are campaigning for a school to remain open, then the fact that your local MP is a former teacher would be very helpful and give you an angle. You may also find a list of their particular policy interests so you know what floats their proverbial boat.

Once armed with this list, you can make your approach. Politicians receive so many requests for help via telephone calls, emails and letters that they tend to prioritise them on a case-by-case basis. In this age of instantaneous communications, email remains the best way to make contact. Not only is it the quickest method, but it offers immediate proof that you sent the request in the first place, rather than be told weeks later that your letter went missing in the internal postal system. You must, however, ensure that your emails are treated as carefully as you would prepare a typed letter. There is no excuse for being so wound up about a particular issue that you send an inappropriate email after a few glasses of wine. One MP told me that he receives more abusive or aggressive messages after 11pm than at any other time of the day.

The days of hardcopy letters are under threat so it probably does not make sense any longer to contact your politicians in this way. The only advantage of this method is that a formal letter makes it slightly more difficult to ignore your request, and usually means a reply in the same format. Older MPs even prefer this method so they can avoid the computer and fax machine.

Contacting your political representatives is easier today than it has ever been. Chances are that your local MP or councillor is signed up to a variety of social networking sites, such as Facebook and Twitter as well as the usual three methods of letter, email and telephone. MPs all share the same postal address which makes it easy to get a letter to them. The standard address is:

[Name] MP, House of Commons, London, SW1A 0AA.

Any letter you send to this address will get to them, as long as you have put the MP's name at the top of the letter.

Telephone contact is also easy, as there is a central switch-board in the Houses of Parliament which you can call and ask to be put through to your MP. The number is 0207 219 3000, but my advice is to only use the telephone in order to chase up an MP who hasn't responded to your request, rather than to use that as the first means of contact. Partly this is just to save you time, given that most PAs will let you ramble on for five minutes before asking you to put everything you have just said into writing.

Email addresses are slightly trickier, as there are two main formats, depending on how long they have been MPs. If your MP was elected before May 2010, it is likely that their address is their surname and first initial @parliament.uk. So Joe Bloggs MP would be bloggsj@parliament.uk. If they were elected more recently, their address is likely to be firstname. lastname.mp@parliament.uk. So Joe Bloggs would be joe. bloggs.mp@parliament.uk. But the easiest and safest way to check is to visit the Parliament website, www.parliament.uk and go to the 'MPs, Lords and offices' section to ensure you get the exact contact details.

Although the parliamentary authorities have taken an age to make it properly accessible, it is a little known fact that you too can go into Parliament and demand to see your MP when the House is sitting. There is an airport-style security operation to endure and occasionally a lengthy wait, but you will get to see your MP eventually, as long as they are in the building that day. You are advised to avoid mid-mornings as they tend to be the busiest time with school visits, and also be aware that MPs are rarely around in the school holidays. Once again, I advise against using this method of contact to initiate a first meeting with your representative, as it is impolite to just pitch up with no prior notice, even if you are part of a larger campaign group. There have been two terrible incidents in the past decade of constituents attack-ing MPs in their local offices, one where a Liberal Democrat MP was attacked with a samurai sword (he survived but his assistant was killed), and the other more recently where a Labour MP was stabbed and had to be rushed to hospital. Unsurprisingly many MPs will therefore be rattled by someone making first contact by simply turning up at Parliament or the constituency office without an appointment.

Recently a senior member of the government, Vince Cable, was embarrassed by a couple of undercover reporters who posed as constituents and got him to reveal some very sensitive information, especially around the activities of media magnate Rupert Murdoch. This might play on some MPs' minds, especially if they are currently ministers. But that is their problem rather than yours, and once you have made contact, and you really want to see the Houses of Parliament for yourself, you should consider trying to get your MP to invite you. It is a real treat even for the most hardened cynic of politics, as you get to see inside this fascinating and grand building; most MPs are rather proud of the place so are happy to give you a whistle-stop tour. As well as a peek into the Chamber to see the famous green benches (if the House of Commons is not sitting), you might get a cup of tea in the Pugin Room, or on the terrace overlooking the Thames. You would be surprised how few individual constituents make such a request, which are not actively encouraged by MPs and their staff who are already contending with a busy diary.

To suggest that you get to know your politicians may be the moment that you begin to question my sanity, as most people in Britain will do anything they can to avoid coming into contact with them, especially around election time. A visit from your local councillor to ask for your vote is considered on a par with discovering the Jehovah's Witnesses at the door.

But if you are going to get the very best out of having elected representatives, then making contact with them is highly recommended. In politics, personal relationships and networking matters a great deal. For a lobbyist or policy adviser it is a useful way of building a profile in Westminster, Edinburgh, Cardiff or Brussels and also aids in understanding how politicians think, what the latest policy trends are, and who is on the rise. Although you will not be competing in this world, taking a brief part of your time to meet your local MP, MEPs and councillor(s) is a worthwhile investment for the future, not least because few people actually do it. The best way to build a network is to do so in 'peacetime', i.e. when you are not actually asking for something in particular, as this helps you to stand out from the crowd when you really need politicians to help you in the future.

Your MP spends a great deal of time in Westminster during the week but begins to travel back on Thursday (especially if they represent a constituency in the far reaches of the country), usually devoting Friday to meet with constituents in his or her local office. This is your best and most appropriate chance to see them face to face. Of course, they could try to turn down your offer for a coffee, but they can never be quite sure who they may have slighted. I know an MP who, as a candidate in a marginal constituency, simply took the approach of accepting every single invite made to them in case they upset someone influential. It was doubtless exhausting but they succeeded in getting enough votes to be elected, so surely worthwhile. At a local level, everyone knows someone who knows someone. As I have said before, MPs have become increasingly risk-averse because of the expenses scandal and the resulting public outcry, so they are treating every single request they receive very carefully.

Although it will differ from individual to individual, the likelihood is that your MP will give you 20–30 minutes to meet. You can always demand to see them in Parliament, but sticking with the local area is definitely the best way to proceed, not least because it will be more convenient for you and them. Although they are busy people, it's best to use the tactic of suggesting an informal cup of tea or coffee for no more than twenty minutes. This works for a number of reasons. Firstly, it is very difficult for an MP to claim that there is no opportunity whatsoever to meet with you at all in the course of a few months, given that you are asking for so little of their time. Not even the Prime Minister's diary is that full (although unless you are a constituent of the Oxfordshire town of Witney, do not waste your time trying). Secondly, pitching it as 'informal' signals to the MP that they just have to come along and listen, rather than have to read weighty briefing material and initiate research in advance. Nor will it set off alarm bells that the person they are meeting is going to simply rant for the duration of the meeting. This technique of coaxing an MP into meeting you rarely fails but it always amazes me how few people adopt it. Even in my line of work, people write to MPs demanding hour-long meetings with a full agenda of topics to discuss – an approach which usually ends in abject failure.

When you finally get a date in the diary, you should bear in mind that it doesn't really matter what your politics are. Whether you're a Conservative, a Labour supporter or a Liberal Democrat, you should view your MP as a route to getting what you want even if you do not agree with their broader policy outlook. When you meet the MP in question, just introduce yourself, remain polite, and discuss any local (or national) issues which might be on your mind. You should then explain why you want to keep in touch: say that you understand that he or she has big issues and important decisions to focus on, but that you are likely to ask them for help from time to time. The most likely help will be in relation to your battles as both a consumer and community campaigner. If you have not already gathered the information, do ask what the preferred method is for contacting the office, who the best contact would be, and try to get a direct dial phone number. Make sure you take a note of the name of your MP's constituency and Westminster secretaries. From my experience they are often as powerful as their boss. They act as the gatekeeper between you and the MP, and are fully aware of their power to veto or delay meetings, so it pays to be nice.

One issue to be wary of is that constituents proactively

contacting an MP without a burning issue is so unusual that they might suspect that you want to become involved with the party locally. Few of us are loyal to any particular political persuasion these days, so do not feel pressured into becoming a party member or delivering leaflets unless you really want to. As an aside, I know someone who does deliver leaflets for a political party not because they care about what materials they are delivering, but because they find it an invaluable way of losing winter weight with the brisk exercise it offers.

During the course of your introductory meetings, especially with MPs, you should make it clear that you might require their help now and then in consumer disputes or local campaigns. Make clear that this does not mean you will need them to chase every company with which you have a customer services issue, but that copying the MP's name into email or letter correspondence is sometimes enough to make a difference. That will also assuage their fears that their role as an MP is going to be relegated to a mixture of social worker and Citizens Advice Bureau. You will find that MPs generally will be pleased to be seen to have helped in some way, especially if they do not actually have to make a great deal of effort in doing so. In return it is possible that they might ask if you would be willing to be mentioned anonymously in one of their constituency newspapers, praising the help you received. There is usually no harm in doing this but ultimately you can say no if you are uncomfortable in doing so.

Now that you are prepared to meet your MP and know who to write to, you will need some appropriate text which explains the purpose of your contact. The letter might read:

Dear Mr/Mrs [Name] MP,

I am one of your constituents, living in [insert name of council ward/name of street]. Although I do not have a specific issue to raise with you at this time, I would like the opportunity for a short, informal meeting during one of your upcoming Friday surgeries. I believe it is important for residents to meet and get to know their Member of Parliament given the number of important issues on which you represent us. If a meeting is convenient, please do not hesitate to contact me on either tel: XXX or email: XXX.

Kind regards, Joe Bloggs.

Providing your full contact details, especially your postal address, will help to confirm that you live in the constituency.

As I have mentioned previously, MPs are busy and the communications which they receive are relentless. That said, you should not have to wait weeks for a response, so mark a date in the diary when you would expect to have heard from them (a gap of no more than ten days after the original request was sent is probably fair). If you are sending a further email, forward on your original request, as this acts as a record and reminder of your original message. If you telephone, please make sure you have the details of when and how you made the request to help the PA or researcher find out what the next steps are, but hopefully this will not be necessary and a meeting/answer to your query can be returned to you swiftly. In regards to an actual face-to-face meeting, you should expect any agreed date to be at least a few weeks into the future, as the window of opportunity to meet your MP will be small, especially for a Friday surgery.

How NOT to contact your MP
You may dislike politicians generally or your local MP specifically, but you must always avoid being aggressive when you make contact with them. Many people do not understand the difference between being assertive and being rude, but you must always uphold the best possible behaviour in order to get what you want.

When people feel powerless and helpless, they often feel stressed, and resentment builds towards the person or persons who are deemed to be preventing a situation being resolved in the way they wish. But the moment you lose your cool, or make unreasonable demands upon a politician, you give them a way out of helping you at all. In your own personal or work life you would not accept being shouted at by a friend or a customer, so expect politicians to adopt the same attitude too. This does not mean being passive or apologetic, just firm but fair.

One man who got his political contact very wrong was Bryan Haven, an anti-mast campaigner in London who was convicted in April 2010 for causing 'annoyance, inconvenience or anxiety' after sending Mayor Boris Johnson over thirty emails. He had good reason to be upset, given that Transport for London had erected a 60 foot mast outside his house. However, sending abusive messages directly to the Mayor's office was entirely the wrong approach. By resorting to the email equivalence of violence, it allowed the Mayor's team to cry foul and make the inappropriate placement of the mast a secondary issue. The protestor was sentenced to community service and a two-year restraining order, banning him from making any contact with the Mayor.

Another thing unlikely to catch the eye of your MP in a positive way are the round-robin postcards and template letters produced by pressure groups, charities, and environmental protestors which you may be asked to sign every now and then. You might get an email from an interest group you belong to, or get collared by someone running a stand in the high street. You might be asked to fill out an online form which then transmits a standard message to a secretary of state, or even to every MP in the House of Commons. This type of approach makes MPs apoplectic with rage, and not because you have them on the run. It is because such communication is so lazy and impersonal. In turn, the responses from MPs will be produced en masse in a similar fashion by the party's headquarters. This means that the MP is not really thinking hard about the issues that the round-robin has highlighted, and everyone's time has been wasted. It also damages the brand of the organisation which you are supporting, and can therefore be detrimental to the issues that you care about in the longer term.

I have a great deal of sympathy with the view of politicians that round-robin letters are annoying. If people cannot be bothered to email or write personally, to nuance their call to action, then how much do they actually care about the issue? I have never yet signed such a postcard and never would, because I would rather spend fifteen minutes on my laptop writing and sending my own email which I have carefully drafted. An individual letter will get an individual response, whereas a template question will get a template answer.

It is a similar principle with petitions. How many times have you signed a petition and seen evidence that it has made a single iota of difference? In fact, many people get disengaged from community campaigns because they see little result from the numerous petitions they have signed over the years. They come to assume that such campaigns cannot be won, and switch off from the political process entirely. Groups which ask you to sign a petition often go for a high number of signatures, targeting quantity over quality which is always the wrong approach in a campaign. A list of random people on a piece of paper can never match a considered, well-argued set of reasons why something should be permitted or stopped. The only caveat to this point is that a petition used for the purposes of a photo opportunity can sometimes be of use, with the pages fanned out and held by the local MP or councillor. I once used a similar technique for a petition to help save a local post office, taking a photo of the slips being handed to my local MP outside the entrance to the House of Commons and it featured in the local newspaper. There is also the classic image of a delegation of campaigners delivering a weighty box or two of signed petitions to 10 Downing Street, although you need permission in advance to get access to this tightly controlled area. But all this is a lot of effort to go to for a single photo, when you could be spending time doing other things of greater use.

From a campaign's perspective there is also the benefit of petitions helping to develop a new list of potential supporters (as long as you remember to provide a box for their postal or email address). But in any given consultation the number of signatories on a petition is usually futile. After many years of local authorities and private companies receiving numerous petitions, especially opposition to planning applications, they have formulated a system where even a petition with 500 carefully listed names will only be considered as one objection. It is therefore much better to send individually composed letters and force them all to be read and considered.

One of the most heinous crimes you can commit when dealing with a politician is to purposely withhold information when asking them to pursue your case. If you persuade your MP to stand up and speak out on your behalf, and they subsequently discover something which you had not willingly told them, your credibility will be shot to pieces. Some people assume that people who work in public relations and the media lie all the time in the course of their work. That is simply not true, especially as there is a clear disincentive in doing so. Once you are considered a liar or at best disingenuous, your battered reputation will spread and you are unlikely to be fully trusted again, thereby hampering your career. I guess politicians are especially sensitive to this given so many of them have been caught out saying things which prove not to be true. You might recall the sad case of former Conservative Cabinet minister Jonathan Aitken who brought a libel action against *The Guardian* newspaper and promised 'to cut out the cancer of bent and twisted journalism in our country with the simple sword of truth and the trusty shield of British fair play'. Of course, it turned out that *The Guardian*'s story was correct, and Aitken eventually went to jail.

I'm sure you are waiting for a 'but' and an excuse for not always fully revealing your hand and I will accept that there is one small caveat. Put simply, it is not that sensible to answer questions which have not actually been asked of you. What I mean by this is that you are not compelled to provide information which has not been requested. It is up to the person challenging you to ask the right questions, and you also have every right to present your case in the best possible light. That is what we all do when we write our curriculum vitae. A CV is not there for you to present the things you cannot do, but rather to showcase what you can do.

If you are simply presenting the very best argument to a politician they will understand that they are getting one particular view of an issue. MPs do this all the time too, as an opposition party will attack a tax increase levied by the government of the day even if privately they accept that they would have to do the same. Or they will stretch and make the very best of the statistics available to increase the pressure. It is not lying or being deceitful, it is just the nature of modern political discourse. If you were to ask a right-winger and a left-winger what they thought of former Prime Minister Margaret Thatcher, the former would say she saved Britain from a sad, seemingly inevitable social and economic decline; the latter would say she helped to tear apart the social fabric of the country, especially targeting the working classes. It's not that one of these views is correct and the other not. They are simply exaggerated and loaded positions expressed by two groups with very different perceptions of that era.

If you contact an MP about keeping a post office counter open, then it is not your job to explain the cost-saving benefits to Royal Mail, or acknowledge that there are alternatives nearby. You are making the case as to why it needs to stay open for the good of the community and local businesses. Similarly, if you are campaigning against a mobile phone mast near to your house, it is not your job to acknowledge its potential usefulness for those with mobile phones. Leave a balanced argument to the local papers rather than trying to take on that task yourself because you can be certain that your opponent(s) will be making a partisan case to their political audiences.

MEPs *and councillors*

It is inevitable that the majority of this book focuses on the relationship with your local MP, given their influence on your day-to-day life. But it is also worth being aware of the other people that you elect, knowing what they do and how to contact them.

As you may be aware, the UK is split into 650 parliamentary constituencies. Each constituency elects one person to represent them, and the political party which wins the most constituencies gets the right to form a government. Sometimes a party wins by a landslide, as Margaret Thatcher did in 1983 or as Tony Blair did in 1997, but a rare event happened in May 2010 when the biggest party, the Conservatives, had to forge a coalition with the Liberal Democrats to give them a working majority.

The European Parliament is a whole different beast. Rather than have single representatives for a specific town or city, the European electoral system means that Members of the European Parliament (MEPs) are elected to cover regions of the UK, such as London, the South-East, and the North-West. Each political party has to produce a list of the candidates for each region, which are numbered. Depending on the final share of the vote, a specific number of candidates for each party will be sent to Brussels to represent us.

On the one hand it would be ridiculous to have 650 MEPs for the UK (especially as that number would be multiplied by the twenty-six other EU member states), but the downside of this system is the lack of proper representation. You do not even choose a specific candidate, as each party provides a list drawn up by its members. The role of an MEP is also very different to their equivalents in Westminster, not least because they have to travel a great deal between the UK, Brussels and Strasbourg. This makes them even more difficult to track down in person, although they are responsive to electronic communications.

So their presence is less tangible, less obvious and therefore people inevitably wonder what they do all day. It is unlikely that you will be able to name a single UK MEP, although occasionally an individual such as the Conservative Daniel Hannan does something newsworthy, such as his brutal verbal bashing of Gordon Brown's handling of the economy which became a global YouTube sensation[1]. But generally they have to fight hard to get noticed at all. Broadly speaking MEPs have the powers to approve, amend or reject most of European legislation, but only collectively with loosely aligned colleagues across national borders. They hold the European Commission to account and can, in theory, force it to resign. The European Parliament also helps decide the way the EU budget is spent, and at which levels.

MEPs tend to be mavericks in comparison to their Westminster counterparts, partly because the parties put people on the list who best reflect their views on the European Union. They are usually either vehement Eurosceptics or strong supporters of the European project. They are also less under the spotlight too which makes it slightly more difficult to pressure them, especially as they are not directly elected.

However, the big downside to being an MEP is the lack of attention they get. Even the most humble Westminster backbencher gets their moment in the sun from time to time, but European representatives can literally spend four years in Brussels without a single mention of their work in the UK press. This can be very frustrating, especially if they also have designs on a seat in the House of Commons. It is quite common for those with parliamentary ambitions to first get elected as an MEP, with notable examples including Deputy Prime Minister Nick Clegg and his Cabinet colleague Chris Huhne.

UK MEPs also get scant attention from their own party hierarchies, partly because out of sight means out of mind.

---

1. http://www.danielhannanmep.com/

It is surprising in one sense, given that so much of the UK's laws and taxes come from Brussels, but MEPs remain second class citizens in the political world. This often means that UK MEPs try to find a small issue which might garner them some coverage and respect, given that the macro issues are so difficult to influence in the vastness of the Brussels debating chamber. An example of a campaign highlighted by UK MEPs was the opposition of the Food Supplements Directive (2002). The dietary supplements industry in the UK strongly opposed the Directive, as did a large number of consumers throughout Europe, including over one million in the UK, and many doctors and scientists, who opposed it on the grounds of unjustified restrictions of consumer choice.

Although they are less useful than their Westminster counterparts to your community campaigns, MEPs are generally hungry for an issue which they could get involved with. So do consider whether you can use them in an appropriate way to build and develop your campaign strategy. Contacting MEPs is relatively easy, via the usual three methods of telephone, letter or email. In order to find out the names and contact details of the MEPs for your region, you need to check via the European Parliament's website which will provide you with a postal address, email and telephone number.

Getting in touch with your councillor(s) is even easier. In some cases where you might have three representatives, you might want to be choosy about which ones you meet. In some instances there might be a party split, i.e. you might have two Conservative councillors and one Labour. In that instance, if you can bear it, you might decide it is worth meeting a representative of each party so you can get them competing with one another to help you. In the case of a councillor it is perfectly reasonable to request that they come and visit you at your home, as they are likely to live within a mile or two. If you have a planning issue, or a concern about speeding on a particular main road, you should ask them to meet you at the site so they can see the problem for themselves.

Many councillors are retired men and women who are winding down from their main careers, and want to give something back to their community. A growing number, however, also have day jobs and young families. Given that politics has become a career to many graduates and young professionals, having something tangible on the CV which demonstrates their political experience and commitment could help them in the future. For those who are younger, it can be extremely tough. I served for four years at borough council level and found it difficult to balance a very busy day job and a family with being a councillor too. You end up dealing with constituency complaints and queries during your lunch break, or sneaking off out of the office like a secret smoker to make phone calls. As for local council meetings, they can be dull, full of procedure, and designed for folk who have nothing better to do with their time than debate a spelling error in paragraph 32c. I once found myself in a 30-minute debate about whether a sentence contained a split infinitive. So do try to be more understanding with councillors than you are with other elected politicians, given that they are usually folk with a day job and family, and are doing this unglamorous job out of civic duty.

The role of a councillor varies according to which area they represent. Being a councillor in a London borough or on Birmingham City Council for example is a big deal as the budgets they control are huge, and their powers are varied. They manage nearly all local services. In Manchester, for example, the total annual budget is an eye-watering £500 million. At the other extreme, being a district councillor in a sleepy Essex village is much less demanding, and carries fewer responsibilities which include council tax and refuse. Most of the time, however, they will be asked by local people in their wards to object to a planning application or get improved recycling facilities for the area. But they do also have a say in bigger issues such as setting council tax rates for the next year, or spending money in your community. With a greater emphasis on 'localism' in British politics, we can expect the role of a councillor to become a more attractive proposition, as long as the coalition delivers on its promise to transfer decision-making powers from central government to local communities.

At a small authority few can devote their full time to it, unless they are retired and are a Cabinet member or are especially passionate about the role. At a larger council, there are people who can make it pay well enough in allowances to treat it as a full time job. If you are the leader of Birmingham City Council, you will be earning more money than a Member of Parliament, and arguably making more significant decisions.

If we accept that there is a variation in the quality of MPs in Parliament, then this is multiplied many times over at a local government level. There are some councillors in the UK who are genuinely first-rate campaigners, running exciting and innovative projects, whilst keeping taxes low for local people and businesses. There are others who care deeply about the communities in which they live and are proud to represent it, and have not come from high-powered day jobs but are cleaners, shop workers, or work for charities. The best thing about local government is the mix of people who get involved; the worst thing is that it does also attract strange obsessives who set out to oppose every development, every minor change to the community and are hugely out of touch with the modern world. The average age of a councillor in the UK is fifty-nine, and this often means that there is a strong vein of 'small c' conservatism which runs through many local authorities, finding it difficult to adapt to the new and emerging needs for groups such as teenagers. It is natural for an older councillor to find it difficult to understand the need or benefit of a skate park, for example, if they do not understand what purpose it serves.

Councillors, just like MPs and MEPs, want to remain elected. The urge to retain a local ward perhaps is not as strong as for an MP who relies on winning for a career, but it is still very much present. A reasonable proportion of defeated councillors try again, where the vanquished are less tarnished than their Westminster counterparts. In summary you should involve them in your community campaigns as they will continue to be a useful additional support, especially if you need to influence council officials as part of your efforts.

In order to contact your local councillor you will need to go via your local council website. County councillors and borough councillors will be on different sites, but on each one just look out for 'Council and Democracy' or some such heading to lead you to your local representative. Some of them are even open enough to list their home address, telephone numbers and occasionally their mobile numbers too. Also look out for the leaflets they will put through your door from time to time, as they often contain a handy contact box for all of your locally elected politicians.

The new relationship

Despite the prospect of a nail-bitingly close general election in 2010, turnout barely rose from 2005. In 1992, nearly eight out of ten of us voted, but this has fallen to a miserly 65 per cent. At a time when millions of people vote for reality TV stars, genuine participation in public policy issues is plummeting, with no sign that we have yet hit the bottom.

In conversations with family and friends, many of whom are not interested in politics, I am struck by how few people are aware of the changes which have been implemented to tighten the system of expenses and allowances. According to them, MPs are still earning a small fortune. So for all of the investigations, the agonising, and leaders competing to see who can be the meanest to their own parties it has led to very little improvement in the trust and perception we have of the new intake of 2010.

The message is clear: the faces may change, but politicians are all the same. The scandal over MPs' expenses has not irrevocably broken our relationship with elected politicians, but it has certainly changed its nature for a very long time. Now that the dust has begun to settle, we have concluded that we now expect them to do more, for less. MPs have no hand to play in this new game – they cannot tell their constituents to go away and stop bothering them – so the key is to understand how to make the most of it. Of course, public opinion still accepts that politicians do important work, representing us on issues in the UK, EU and even the local town hall. But MPs are very close to alienating the public entirely, and next time it might be irreversible.

Although we have never exactly loved MPs, public opinion towards them changed remarkably quickly after the *Telegraph* began publishing the expenses data. A major report published in December 2010 found four in ten people no longer trusted politicians to put the national interest first and the majority of voters believed MPs never told the truth. The study, charting social attitudes over the last three decades, found that mistrust in politics was now four times higher than it was in the mid-1980s.

Researchers from the national centre for social research insisted confidence in the political system had never been particularly high but the MPs' expenses scandal appeared to have 'helped erode trust yet further'. Four in ten people 'almost never' trust governments of any party to put the national interest first, up from the previous all-time high of 34 per cent.

However, this distrust is only partly due to the recent expenses scandal. It has been on the cards for many years as society has become disillusioned by the nature of our politics and the succession of broken promises. We also 'consume' politics in an entirely different way, less based on inherited loyalties and more likely to be driven by what we can get in return for our votes. Modern voters often treat politicians as they would a broadband provider or mobile phone operator that wants our business.

This competitive spirit is ever more apparent in politics, and constituents are much less content to allow an MP to sit back and relax until a few weeks before the next election. Therefore, if we are to have a new and improved relationship with politicians, you should harness their desire to please you: a reversal of the way they have tended to use you for your vote in the past. This means contacting them when you need them, and at the time most difficult for them to say no. Election time is the perfect opportunity to play politicians off against one another, all in pursuit of your vote, and not just to mend streetlights and broken paving slabs, but in your everyday battles as a consumer, as a parent, and as a taxpayer.

Politicians exist today in an environment where politics is a buyers' market, and saying no is a high risk strategy for them as they are ultimately at your electoral beck and call. The expenses scandal described at the beginning of this chapter has only increased politicians' sense of unease about their long time chances of survival, making them more risk-averse than ever.

This new relationship need not be a bad thing for politicians either. It does mean that they will need to spend more time on the micro issues, rather than the national and global, but the reward will be to increase their profiles in the community. By standing up for their constituents either passively or actively against poor corporate or public sector behaviour, citizens will at least see the benefit of having an MP. They might even see them as good value for money, which the polls tell us is not currently the case.

I am not advocating that you passively sit back and hope that your MP will help you in your hour of need. You will need to push and cajole them into being helpful, by understanding their pressure points, fears and concerns. This requires some effort on your part but far less than you would imagine.

Chapter 2: Corporates

We are all short of time, and we just want things to work. We have families to care for, jobs to go to and bills to pay. Yet the whole time we are having to battle with companies to get a basic level of service. Our interactions with the commercial world can be extremely frustrating and polls suggest that our trust in companies to do the right thing is now at an all-time low. Nothing quite works the way it should, and it places unnecessary pressures and stresses upon citizens. In the process of writing this book I asked people to send me examples of situations which frustrate them. They include:

›   At the post office, you queue for hours just to get a parcel or letter sent. You have to pay extra to be sure that your mailing will get there by the next day, even though that was what a first class stamp was presumably designed for. The cost of posting things increases each year, but the reliability of the post seemingly decreases.

›   Gas and electricity companies advise you to pay by direct debit, and persuade you to make the monthly figure higher than your usage just to be sure. When the company realises that they have overcharged, you get a letter informing you that they owe you money but have decided to take it off future bills instead. Leaving aside the benefit to the company of holding on to this extra cash, when is a customer permitted to delay payment on a whim?

› Budget airlines that charge you for every last thing they can get away with, such as checking-in a bag, or for a drink of water on the flight. Bear in mind that the chief executive of Irish carrier Ryanair even tried to charge passengers to go to the toilet. It cannot be long before there is an additional charge for the plane to have wings.

› Train companies which increase the cost of your annual season ticket by two or three times the rise of inflation, or provide a confusing range of different ticket prices. When you do get on the train, you might be breezily informed that your services have been cancelled or they cram you in like sardines.

These are just some examples of everyday frustrations. There is just a sense that nothing quite works as it should. When you find good customer service you want to cry with happiness and hug the individual who is being helpful, because it is so rare. Incidentally, do make sure you show your appreciation to companies when things go well, as we need there to be an incentive for people to do the right thing.

What's the problem?

A poll[2] in May 2010 found that politicians are not trusted to defend consumers' rights. Senior politicians such as the Prime Minister David Cameron and his Deputy Prime Minister Nick Clegg, received no votes at all in the poll; nor did the Office of Fair Trading (OFT), an organisation whose raison d'être is to protect consumers. The most trusted site was Money Saving Expert with Tesco, *Which?*, Google, Compare the Market, Facebook and Confused also scoring highly.

---

2. http://www.moneysavingexpert.com/news/family/2010/05/politicians-not-trusted-to-uphold-consumer-rights

What does this tell us? Quite simply that government and politicians have failed to convince consumers that they are on their side. Everything the government does seems pedestrian, lacking user-friendliness and accessibility in comparison to the consumer websites above. With the rise of the iPhone, BlackBerry and other handheld gadgets, you can access sites at home, on the train, and even in the bath (just be careful not to drop it).

In comparison, the political system is nowhere near as flexible and innovative. There is also an inherent criticism of most major corporations in the findings of this poll, namely that the public often do not trust them to provide the best possible price first time. It is not until customers have fully checked what else is available at what price that they commit to buy. Free advice on the internet, however, does appear to instil trust, which is partly why it has driven such fundamental changes in the way we shop over the past fifteen years or so.

You may have seen a movie from the early 1990s called *Falling Down* starring Michael Douglas. Set in Los Angeles, with his marriage and job both coming to a bitter end, the grinding stresses of modern living finally make him crack. Douglas' character, William, enters a fast food restaurant called Whammy Burger and attempts to order breakfast, but he cannot have it because the switch from the breakfast menu to the lunch menu had occurred just three minutes prior to his arrival. After a frustrating argument with the patronising store manager, William draws a sub-machine gun from his bag. Seeing the sheer panic on the faces of the restaurant staff and customers, he decides to order lunch, but takes the staff to task on the difference between the plump, sizzling burger featured on the menu, and the soggy, limp product he gets once he pays.

Now, let us get a few points clear. Firstly, I do not advocate the use of machine guns to settle consumer disputes. Secondly, the character portrayed by Michael Douglas is quite clearly suffering a mental collapse and is therefore not a good role-model for you. But joking aside, the scene identifies the behaviours which drive us all a bit potty. The inflexibility of the rules as applied to the timing of when breakfast is served is something most of us will experience in some form or another. It might be when you attempt to deposit some money into your current account in order to prevent you from going into your overdraft, but discover that you did it five minutes after the cut-off point allowed you to, thus incurring a bank fine. The disappointment of the burger is also something which tells a wider truth about our experience of being a consumer. We are bombarded with clever advertising which seduces us into buying products which are significantly inferior to the way they are depicted on screen or in print.

Why consumers get frustrated

The internet has been a great liberating force, allowing us to access free services, and has increased the availability and transparency of information. The coalition government has even introduced a requirement on local authorities and departments in Whitehall to publish details of what they spend our money on. We can find information quickly and accurately in a matter of seconds. We can buy almost everything online, from our groceries, holidays, clothes and even music, all at the click of a button. We can speak to emigrated relatives by Skype, get back in touch with old friends and colleagues via social networking sites such as Facebook and Twitter, and network professionally at home via LinkedIn. And we can do all of this without even leaving the house.

The downside to this remarkable change in our culture over the past fifteen years is we now expect instant gratification. In other interactions with companies through traditional means, we simply find it hard to get our way. Obstacles are thrown before us to prevent us getting a refund, or our complaints are just ignored. Companies invest millions of pounds on marketing initiatives which claim they have the best customer service, rather than properly training their staff in the first place.

As the internet has speeded up most services in our lives, it feels as though certain sectors have not kept up with the pace. To check your bank account or track a parcel you have posted, the empowerment and convenience for the average consumer has been considerable. But the internet cannot help if your water pipes have burst, or your bill has been wrongly calculated. In those instances you have to call your utility company directly, and inevitably find yourself in a telephone queue that assails your ears with loud music whilst your frustrations build and build.

Like politicians, at least before the current Parliament, corporations give the impression that they would rather expend their energies on creating obstacles for customers than making life easier. This does not work in the long term because consumers are increasingly savvy and, more importantly, they talk to one another. The power of word-of-mouth in both the commercial and political worlds is still grossly underrated, which is why both are increasingly harnessing the power of the internet to create so-called viral campaigns. If a friend sends you details of a product or service, you are more likely to try it than if you are informed by a standard advertising campaign.

The coalition government is moving in the right direction by making a lot of information available to its own customers (i.e. its citizens) about how government spends money and how decisions are made. But some people do not trust government to reveal the really interesting information, and have taken it upon themselves to do so. It does point to a bigger problem for governments and companies, namely how to retain secrecy and privacy when one person who is willing to risk information gathering or leak internal documents can disseminate it across the world to millions of people at the press of a button. As stated in the previous chapter, when Parliament tried to prevent full information of MPs' expenses from being available to the public, it was simply put onto a disk and handed over to a national newspaper to publish.

The ensuing coverage was then shared around the world in a matter of seconds.

In the public sector things get even worse. Council tax levels B and D in England have risen exponentially over the past fifteen years from an average of £609 in 1995 to £1,439 in 2010, yet what we get in return feels as though it has diminished. Bin collections are less frequent in many parts of the country, and at the first sign of snow on the ground, the trucks park up and have a tea break. If you complain, health and safety laws are cited (despite the fact that YOU manage to get to work). The quality of state schools and hospitals has improved in recent years but by a tiny proportion compared with the extra money we have been spending on them. This is why many people get frustrated and angry about their taxes, not because they believe they should not have to contribute, but that the return on the investment is often so disappointing. We might all know that the person on the front desk at your local Town Hall effectively works for you as a local taxpayer, but you are left under no illusions as to who considers themselves to be the boss.

Generally speaking, consumers get a bad deal in their everyday relationship with the commercial world. If you are unhappy with your high street bank's policy on overdraft charges, what in all honesty can you do about it? Most people live permanently in their overdrafts, so cannot afford to move accounts. There is very little variety in the marketplace, as most banks charge similar amounts and moving current accounts is a tortuous process, with direct debits and other information having to be changed.

Faced with these hurdles, most people do not bother, and therefore lose money in the process. Do not forget too that every time you fill out a mortgage application form you will be asked how long you have been with your bank, which indicates that you are rewarded, in relation to the credit check agencies, by sticking with the same bank you chose on your eighteenth birthday. Many of us choose our bank in our teenage years on the basis of a free gift being offered rather than taking a sensible long-term view.

It seems that companies have to be dragged into doing the right thing; once there is a financial incentive or imperative to change, they do. But many corporates spend an inordinate amount of time fighting their customers with small print rules which prevent refunds, or trying their luck with higher prices which they hope you do not notice. When was the last time the standard insurance on your home and possessions actually got cheaper, without switching to another provider? You have not made a single claim, have had better locks fitted on doors and windows, the crime rate has not increased locally, and yet you get hit by a 20 per cent plus increase the next year as your reward.

Companies work on the basis that apathy will always win. You might not like the service you receive but you cannot be bothered to do anything about it. The public's attitude towards corporations is increasingly similar to its one on the main political parties, namely that they let you down, they do not listen, and they do not change.

If we do not like the antics of the people who represent us in Westminster, we can actively choose not to participate, namely not bother to vote and switch off the television every time the Prime Minister appears. But you cannot choose to live in a house without heating, electricity or water nor can you (unless you are Roman Abramovich) travel without going to an airport and using an airline. Avoiding bad politicians is relatively easy, but avoiding bad companies is less so.

One of the most important, and often overlooked, parts of planning a campaign is to consider exactly who you are up against, which battles you are unlikely to win, and which you can. When you take on a major company, the voice you often hear at the other end of the line is probably sat in a call centre, and it is therefore easy to underestimate the extent of the challenge you are facing.

The loss of faith in big business

Despite the efforts to reassure the public, it is likely that we will retain our distrust of the political classes for many more years to come. Reputations will not be turned around overnight. But politicians are not the only major group in our lives to have let us down.

For many years, we have looked on in awe at the growth of certain companies and brands, and their ability to use their collective ingenuity to generate wealth, prosperity and employment. Think back to the formation of companies such as Ford in the US and Cadbury's in the UK. Both were set up to improve the lot of the people working for the companies: Henry Ford pioneered 'welfare capitalism' and introduced the $5-per-day wage which doubled that earned by most of his workers, whilst John Cadbury pioneered pension schemes for his employees.

But in recent decades, major abuses, mainly originating in the United States, have helped to create a lack of trust and general cynicism towards the whole corporate sector. In truth, we have become almost as sceptical about it as we have about politicians.

There are two particular instances in the previous decade which have fostered this belief that big business is not to be trusted. They are by no means the only abuses which have taken place, but they have become representative of the wider malaise.

Enron

This Texan-based energy provider hit the headlines in late 2001 when the seemingly invincible company suffered a fatal financial collapse. It was partly blamed on dodgy accounting practices which had kept many millions of dollars of debt off its balance sheet.[3]

Everything had seemed rosy just months before. Perceived as a shining example of the power of corporate America,

3. http://news.bbc.co.uk/1/hi/business/1780075.stm

Fortune magazine tipped the company to keep growing and was therefore one of the safest stocks for investors. It had won several awards such as 'America's most innovative company' for six consecutive years. And not only did it wow the financial markets, but Enron's senior executives were also regularly courted by the White House for advice on energy policy. In return, they also made generous contributions to the President's inauguration fund.

In just fifteen years, Enron had come from nowhere to being the seventh biggest company in the world's most powerful economy. But what was uncovered in the run-up to its collapse sent shockwaves across the world. In short, the firm's success turned out to be nothing but an elaborate scam. Enron executives had repeatedly lied about how much money it was making, and in the process covered up much of its debt. As the full extent of the scam became clear, it created huge panic and the company was plunged into bankruptcy.

In case you think that white collar criminals always escape justice, you will be pleased to know that there was no such leniency shown to Enron's senior executives. One, the former chief executive Jeff Skilling, was sentenced to more than twenty-four years in prison, and given a fine of $45 million. But although justice was done, the implications of this scandal still reverberate today. This, and other similar incidents, led to strict new corporate rules being introduced. More importantly, though, the public lost faith in major corporations and polling demonstrates that they continue to distrust their motives.

The bankers

Although Enron became a byword for corporate scandal, its impacts were generally contained within the United States. New rules came into place which were perceived to have helped restore some public faith in corporate behaviour. But a crisis was about to emerge which would put the effects of Enron firmly into the shade.

In brief, the beginning of the last decade saw interest rates in the United States fall to their lowest for many years, to just 1 per cent. The low interest rate encouraged people to buy property, and this in turn persuaded mortgage lenders to offer money to people who would usually be excluded from borrowing. These borrowers tended to be people with bad credit ratings and were usually on low incomes. Unsurprisingly, this market was extremely popular, because as in the UK most people see property as an investment which can only increase in value over time.

The people given the task of selling these financial products worked on commission. Therefore, they had no further responsibility to the borrower once the papers had been signed. However, a couple of years into the agreement, these new homeowners suddenly saw their repayment costs rise sharply. The introductory rate came to an end and interest rates began to rise again to their natural level, which inevitably led to people defaulting on their mortgage payments, which in turn cost the lenders. Usually, a mortgage lender can recoup its losses by taking possession of the property and re-selling it. But because there were so many properties being sold, and falling demand, the lenders were only getting a fraction of its outlay back. The boom had firmly come to an end, and house prices went into freefall.

So what? Yes, people lost their homes and had lost any hope of owning property again in the future. But at least the irresponsible lenders also suffered too, and some have gone out of business. Well, it is not that simple, and this is the reason why it has affected us in the UK too. In order to raise the money to lend to the subprime market, mortgage companies had themselves borrowed from financial institutions. By selling mortgage debt to banks, they were effectively sharing the risk and insuring themselves. This meant that established global financial institutions were knowingly, or sometimes unknowingly, saddled with toxic debt too.

The problem was covered up for so long because the banks

which had shared the risk with the mortgage lenders were some of the biggest and most trusted names in the business, such as Lehman Brothers and Morgan Stanley. The whole enterprise came to a grinding halt when the number of defaults rapidly grew and the major banks realised the extent of their exposure. The 'bad' debt was so eye-wateringly high that it led to the unthinkable. In 2008 the fourth largest investment bank in the United States, Lehman Brothers, filed for bankruptcy. But unlike Enron, the impacts of this crisis touched every person on the planet.

The continuing row over the extent to which irresponsible bankers are being rewarded for their previous risk taking shows no sign of abating. On the one hand it is perfectly logical to argue that bankers will need to continue to be well paid in order to be incentivised to make the UK's nationalised banks even more profitable and therefore more attractive to potential buyers. But on the other hand, you can understand the public's reaction to multimillion pound bonuses being given to people who are perceived to have made the mistakes in the first place. This is especially true when the taxpayers who helped to bail out the ailing banks are themselves suffering a freeze on their pay or even redundancy.

Why do companies lose touch?

When companies are too big they become like huge sea vessels that take an age to turn around or change course. They still have the weight and ability to crush those hit, but smaller and more nimble competitors can challenge their very existence. Companies lose touch because they often do not have strong incentives to provide a better service if there are a lack of genuinely influential voices holding them to account. Companies become self-absorbed and grow their internal bureaucracies, creating multiple posts for the same task, and lose sight of the reason for their very existence which is to provide a service which is designed to make money for its owners.

Although it sometimes seems that way, companies do not

set out to alienate their customers, but there must be a reason why big companies witness a fall in standards. More than at any point in our history we are driven by and attracted to brands in our day-to-day decisions. Brand loyalty means that we are willing to drive the extra two or three miles to visit a McDonald's restaurant rather than a Burger King; it means we will wait an extra week for furniture from IKEA than go to the Habitat down the road. Brands make themselves a part of your life through an intense competition driven by marketing and advertising. Any advertising expert will tell you that the key is to get people to buy not on the basis of the actual product, but on the basis of the lifestyle choice it signifies. Using the examples from a moment ago, many of us are disappointed by what we actually get back in return, yet we stay loyal.

In a spoof television advert for Coca-Cola, featured in the film *The Invention of Lying*, the representative of the company appears on screen and declares the following:

> Hi, I'm Bob. I'm the spokesperson for the Coca-Cola company. I'm here today to ask you to continue buying coke. Sure it's a drink you've been drinking for years, and if you still enjoy it, I'd like to remind you to buy it again sometime soon. It's basically just brown sugar water, we haven't changed the ingredients much lately, so there's nothing new I can tell you about that. We changed the can around a little bit though. See, the colours here are different there, and we added a polar bear so the kids like us. Coke is very high in sugar and like any high calorie soda it can lead to obesity in children and adults who don't sustain a very healthy diet. So that's it, it's coke. It's very famous, everyone knows it. I'm Bob, I work for coke, and I'm asking you to not stop buying coke.

In reality, the product means much more than that to many millions of loyal customers around the world. For some, the Christmas holidays have not begun until the seasonal advert 'Holidays are Coming' is on our screens. The advantage of a product such as Coke is that its basic ingredients stay the same. Whether you are drinking it in Taiwan or Torquay, it will taste the same. Whether you are entering a McDonald's in Rome or Rochdale, the experience and food will broadly be the same. But in other companies, the reputation of the brand can change from day to day. If you are on a Eurostar train which leaves on time and gets you to Brussels or Paris comfortably and effortlessly, you will be a very satisfied customer and think well on the company. If there is a delay, even because of something out of control of the company, you will think the opposite. Reputation can be lost in a split second and it is a long road to recovery, so service industries where face-to-face passenger contact is so important need to be especially focused on keeping us all happy.

The biggest brands in our lives today tend to be either long established or more recent, such as the classics Nestlé (1866), Mercedes-Benz (1886), Coca-Cola (1892), Gillette (1895) and Kellogg's (1906). However, the most interesting and exciting brands are often seen to be those which have emerged since the 1990s, such as Amazon.com in 1994, Google in 1998 and Facebook in 2004.

But there is always a peak point when a company is on the up. It's perhaps like our own lives. When we are younger we tend to be more innovative, creative and risk-taking. As we get older we try to consolidate and hold what we already have. When you think about it, some major brands have had to work hard for many years to dwindle the goodwill they used to experience from its customers. British Airways had always held a special place in the hearts of its customers, in its role as the national flag-carrier and its long held position as the most luxurious choice of airline for British passengers. But the aviation market changed radically from the mid-1980s with increased and inspired competition from new players in the long-haul market. Allied to this, a number of 'budget' airlines also emerged, radically cutting the cost of flying short-haul both domestically and nationally. Fuel costs went up, the environmental issues emerged, and the goodwill began to slip away. People still choose BA over other airlines, but the internet has created a more competitive market.

Companies start out as exciting new enterprises, taking on the competition, and changing the game. Think of Richard Branson at Virgin back in the 1970s and 1980s, with his upstart company taking on the record business, and then a national institution such as British Airways. We cheered him on, not because we necessarily preferred his company's product, but because it was exciting to watch. However, such companies eventually lose their sheen, as they become part of the establishment themselves.

But whilst it has taken many decades for the ancient brands to lose some credibility, the newer kids on the block could find themselves losing touch much more quickly. Google's famous founding motto is 'don't be evil', yet there are some critics who argue that its compliance with the internet censorship policies of the Chinese authorities until as recently as March 2010 makes it nearly that. The company has emerged from being just another search engine provider to playing a huge role in our day-to-day lives. To 'Google' is now a verb in itself. Amazon has also come from nowhere to be the favourite internet shopping site in the world. Facebook, in less than a decade, has become an intrinsic way for millions of people around the world interact, so much so that it is reportedly worth around $50 billion.

But what will happen when the company gets too large, employs too many people, becomes less responsive to its users and becomes so mainstream that grandparents now join up? Will Facebook also stop listening to its customers, who will then flee to some other social networking site yet to be created? We have lots of examples of internet brands which suddenly emerge, and fade almost as suddenly. Remember when Friends Reunited seemed so ahead of the game? Barely anyone uses it now. Or how about lastminute.com, once the only place you went to book a late holiday, but now there are hundreds of similar sites offering similar services; or even Napster, the controversial music 'file-sharing' site of the late 1990s, which was eventually shut down.

What makes a CEO tick?

FTSE-100 CEOs are comparable to Premiership football managers as they both oversee huge enterprises, making multimillion pound purchases and decisions, and enjoy large salaries and bonuses in return for success. If they make the right decisions, they are cheered, praised and honoured. And like football managers, CEOs are only one bad decision, one poor year away from being fired. They have to take overall responsibility for errors made by someone working on a factory floor, or on a customer services helpline, even if they have no direct control over them. But sympathy is in short supply for people that can earn £1 million plus per year.

CEOs have to worry about shareholders, regulators, politicians, city analysts, the media, and employees. The demands are huge and diaries are packed. The day can start at 6.30am and finish at 10pm, with late night telephone calls and problems to solve the norm. But they do it because they are driven to succeed; they want to play the game even though the odds are stacked against their long-term survival, just like football managers. Because there is a chance, just a chance, that they might be the one who increases the company's profitability year on year, and can retire at the time of their choosing, with the plaudits ringing in their ears.

It is often assumed that chief executives of Britain's biggest companies are dynamic risk-takers. That is something of a myth. On the one hand, they are undoubtedly successful, often charismatic and intelligent people. To be the figurehead of a multibillion pound company takes something special. But the most dynamic types tend to work for hedge funds, or are old-fashioned entrepreneurs such as Richard Branson. FTSE-100 people have to take more responsibility. They look for 'organic' growth with solid performance and good returns. This is because investors are looking for guaranteed income. This means a well-run business, doing the right thing, and led by a competent and capable CEO. This is especially the case in the field of infrastructure or utilities which are usually regulated in some form, and represent a steady long-term income flow for the investor. These types of companies are especially liked at a time of global economic difficulties, in the same way as you might save your own money in a trusted building society rather than buy shares and take a risk. Regulated utilities are also favoured by the major pension funds which are often looking for low-risk returns, especially since the crazy sub-prime gamble which caused the credit crunch has now come to light.

The days when a company could simply make profit and be lauded for doing so have come to an end. Corporate responsibility and customer service demands means that bottom line profit is becoming inextricably linked with softer skills. Many people shop in Waitrose because the food is sustainably and ethically sourced, and they are willing to pay more for the privilege. They like to recycle, to know the tuna on display did not require cruel netting methods, and to know the number of air miles have been kept to a minimum. It does have to be said that there is still an income divide on the issue of sustainability. High earners have been shown to be willing to pay more in return for better environmental performance, whilst those on the minimum wage are looking for the cheapest price, even if this means buying a battery-farmed chicken.

The need for companies to play it safe and be more sensitive to customer needs gives you an advantage as a consumer or local campaigner. Chief executives are now more risk-averse than ever, careful to protect what they have, and sensitive to criticism.

I recall talking to a senior FTSE-100 chief executive who leads a customer-facing business. In the past, the attitude of the company was not especially geared towards providing support for those who had been unhappy in the service they had received. The previous strategy had been to simply hope the complainant would just go away once he or she had written a couple of letters. But this savvy CEO thought this to be a bizarre attitude. He worried (rightly) that it just takes one tenacious disgruntled customer to get a politician or the media to help their campaign, and the fall out could be significant. Therefore, he simply said to me, 'Why would I risk my company's reputation for the sake of a £200 complaint?' His policy was to shut down and silence the problem before it had the chance to gather momentum. A refund and an apology is a small price to pay to extinguish the threats posed by an irate customer. Most CEOs will feel this way, and that is why the culture of a major company keeps such complaints away from the top brass. Responsibility is therefore delegated for customer complaints down the food chain, with a call centre operative often expected to be the obstinate representative of the company in your dispute.

A great deal of CEOs do not necessarily mind if the company is doing what it can to resist paying off irate customers, because it would impact on the bottom line if they did not. A good example is one of Britain's favourite and most trusted brands, the high street retailer Marks & Spencer. They used to have a refunds policy which meant that a customer could leave it up to ninety days to return an item of clothing, but this was cut back to thirty-five days in 2009. The old policy was clearly too generous and changing the rules was almost certainly on the basis of cost-cutting[4]. But all CEOs dislike direct contact from customers, not just because they do not want to be bothered, but because it demonstrates that the customer services function within the business is not working as it should.

Chief executives of FTSE-100 companies have worked extremely hard to get there. Either they have fought their way from the shop floor, in the case of Terry Leahy at Tesco, or

4. http://www.guardian.co.uk/
money/blog/2009/sep/30/marks-and-spencer-returns-policy

they have a proven track record in getting results, such as Philip Green or Stuart Rose. But now they have got there, they do not wish to relinquish their grip. Yes, even the sack often means a bumper payday but the roles are so high profile that a bad experience could bring to an end a career and a reputation.

The fear of sudden events

There can be no better, or perhaps worse, example of a company taking their brand and trying its hardest to flush it away than BP: one of the world's biggest companies, celebrated by pension-fund managers for its relentless profitability in the days of Blair-favourite Lord Browne, plunged into reputational chaos by its failure to respond effectively to the outcry over the huge oil leak off of the Gulf of Mexico in the early summer of 2010 in an incident President Barack Obama called an 'environmental 9/11'.

What began as a significant challenge to BP soon became a monumental crisis as the company's efforts to quell the leak failed, all under the glare of the watching media. Its then chief executive Tony Hayward became one of the most hated men in the world, especially in the United States, when he told a live television interviewer that 'I just want my life back'. This comment, expressed at a time when millions of gallons of oil were still leaking onto the sea bed, and with eleven people on the rig killed when it exploded, almost singlehandedly ended his tenure as CEO.

Just to compound this error, later in the crisis Hayward took the decision to enjoy an afternoon's sailing with friends just off the south coast. In his defence, the pressure on him must have been beyond any of our comprehension, and he said he had not seen his children for months. But he was spotted and the photograph of an apparently arrogant Brit enjoying a privileged leisure pursuit whilst fishermen in the Gulf of Mexico had seen their livelihoods ruined, played very badly.

The BP incident has spun many senior CEOs into a panic. They watched Tony Hayward and thought 'there but for the grace of God go I'. They have probably spent time thinking about the very worst thing that could happen to their businesses, such as a chemical spill, a plane crash, or an explosion, and what their fate would be if it happened on their watch. Hayward is clearly an intelligent, experienced corporate leader with many skills to offer, but this serious dent to his reputation will take considerable time to clear.

But CEOs are also human beings, usually with families to support and with similar worries and concerns to the rest of us. The money is great, but it is not the primary driver of most people, even at the very top. Their ambition outstrips the desire to earn more money, but they would, of course, be foolish not to ensure they are fairly remunerated. And the sack hangs over them like the sword of Damocles. The companies which they represent are likely to last for several decades, perhaps even hundreds of years. Even BP, for example, will no doubt bounce back from the 2010 oil spill. But a chief executive can be booted out at any point, sometimes for just a single incident which can blindside them in a split second. CEOs live in fear of the sudden event.

Global companies such as McDonald's or Coca-Cola have so much power, both economically and in terms of political influence. However, such companies can only exist with people continuing to buy their products or use their services. It is not impossible for a global brand to fail, or come close to it. Take Coca-Cola, for just under 100 years Coke remained the same wherever you went in the world (geeky fact alert: only the concentrate is produced by the company and distributed under licence to approved manufacturers who then top it up with carbonated water and sweeteners). By spring 1985 Coke had begun to lose its sheen, as younger drinkers seemingly preferred the sweeter taste of Pepsi and previously loyal customers became concerned at Coke's levels of sugar and caffeine. But it was still the biggest-selling soft drink on the planet, and with the minimum amount of customer research and testing they changed the flavour, and renamed it New Coke. The public was not impressed and sales plummeted as the new product was widely boycotted. One of the biggest companies in the world had attempted to force a change upon its customers to suit its corporate strategy to take on Pepsi, and it had failed. Within a few months the traditional version was reintroduced as Classic Coke.

The lesson to take from the story of New Coke is that companies always need to understand their customers if they are going to retain their market position. But not all companies are so easy to punish, especially those which are price regulated. The Coca-Cola Company can only exist as long as people choose to buy its products, but there are some essentials which we have to buy if we want to live, such as water, heating, and electricity. This means there is a different dynamic to the way we complain to regulated companies, than to those which are not.

The car manufacturer Toyota had long enjoyed a reputation for reliability and quality, even being ranked eight on the list of the world's strongest brands in 2009. Within a year, over nineteen fatalities had been attributed to problems with Toyota vehicle acceleration mechanisms, including a tragic crash involving an off-duty California police officer and his family in late August 2009.

The company's worst nightmare has continued to intensify since then. A voluntary recall was announced in November 2009 for owners of certain Toyota and Lexus models. Early the following year Toyota stated it would recall 2.3 million cars to correct sticking accelerator pedals on certain Toyota models and several days later, it decided to suspend sales of eight models.

This respected and established brand suddenly found itself fighting for its very existence and its share price dropped significantly. Car owners remain concerned. Of course, one can point the finger at the chief executive of the company and ask why he did not identify this problem before it caused fatal accidents. But he was not on the factory floor each day personally inspecting vehicles before they were sent out or engaged in the testing procedures. He will have discovered the sudden threat to his business at about the same time as the media, yet was expected to have a solution immediately.

In one of my previous companies, the airports operator BAA, a newly appointed chief executive had been in post for just a matter of weeks. He took the job with a very clear view of his short- and medium-term priorities: an Office of Fair Trading Inquiry which was due to begin later that year about the company's airport ownership; handling reaction to the takeover of the company; and improving the terminal facilities at the airports for passengers. Then in the middle of the night, as he slept soundly at home, his telephone rang. The Home Office, which is responsible for protecting the UK's borders from terrorism, wanted his airports (Heathrow, Gatwick, Stansted, Southampton, Glasgow, Edinburgh and Aberdeen) to dramatically up the stringency of their security checks, beginning in just a few hours. A major bomb plot had been uncovered by the intelligence services, with a group of Islamic extremists attempting to smuggle liquid bombs onto transatlantic planes. In that one telephone exchange, the chief executive will have realised that everything he had been planning to do no longer remained a priority. No company could be reasonably expected to cope with such a sudden and heavy burden placed upon it, and BAA inevitably struggled. You might remember the scenes of long queues of passengers, flights cancelled, and people having to queue and wait in makeshift tents. It was a story made for rolling news coverage, with the airports besieged by journalists, and the company unable to easily solve the problem in the short term. The number of other companies who are susceptible to such commercial catastrophes is huge, and no doubt there are more than a few chief executives who wake up in the morning and wonder if it is their turn next.

Consumer watchdogs

Consumers get frustrated because their product or service-related complaint is ignored, or at least not heard by the people that matter. There is great frustration when there does not appear to be a logical process by which our problems can be satisfactorily resolved. This frustration boils over and leads to the writing of an angry, bile-laden email or letter, or screaming at someone on the telephone. It is understandable, but certainly not productive.

Waiting on a telephone line or in an actual queue can be time-consuming, annoying, and incredibly frustrating. Just imagine how many hours you have spent in the past year waiting in a high street bank, post office queue or on the telephone to your utility companies.

To assist us, a number of so-called consumer watchdogs have been created over time by government, such as Consumer Focus, although this is in the process of being abolished. Watchdogs act as a one-stop shop for disgruntled consumers angry with poor levels of service and bad behaviour from the companies which they encounter. The aspiration of these bodies is to make life easier for the consumer and 'nudge' companies into doing the right thing.

As well as regulators with clear and legally binding powers to attempt to keep certain types of companies in check, the last government also introduced the Enterprise Act (2002) which allowed the Secretary of State for Business, Innovation and Skills to give selected consumer bodies the title of 'super complainant' to the Office of Fair Trading (OFT). This means that they have a much stronger voice and therefore means companies in certain industries have to take them seriously.

These 'super complainants' are intended to 'strengthen the voice of consumers who are unlikely to have access individually to the kind of information necessary to judge whether markets are failing them.' At the time of publication, there are eight bodies which have been approved and given this status.

They are:

- CAMRA: a lobby group which campaigns for higher quality beers.
- The Citizens Advice Bureau (CAB): a free service which provides legal advice, practical help, and information on consumer rights across the country.
- Consumer Council for Water: protects water consumers.
- Consumer Focus: a body funded by the OFT to help consumer resolve complaints (although note that its powers are to be handed over to the CAB).
- General Consumer Council for Northern Ireland: does what it says on the tin.
- National Consumer Council (trading as 'Consumer Focus'): was formed in 2008 but is soon to have its powers stripped and given to the CAB and local trading standards offices.
- The Consumers' Association (trading as *Which?*): a consumer advocacy organisation with substantial powers but which is primarily a lobbying organisation funded by its magazine subscribers.

Everyone should take the time to understand what rights they do and do not have as a matter of course. After all, knowledge is power. A very readable guide can be found on the CAB's website.[5]

Energy is one of the biggest areas represented by such bodies, but everything from the post office to phone charges, to banking and how we are dealt with by the police and other public services is also covered. Consumer Focus claimed it was working with businesses behind the scenes rather than picking public fights, but perhaps that was its ultimate down-

5. www.adviceguide.org.uk

fall. Day-to-day consumer advice is still best represented by the Citizens Advice Bureau, a well-organised and well funded charity. In the instance of energy, Consumer Focus claims that it took on 7,000 cases in 2009, recovering £880,000 in compensation and refunds. Energy complaints can include hard-sell tactics from doorstep salesmen, high prices, and firms disconnecting needy customers. The head of the body even claimed he could prove the power of smart complaining, by taking on his energy company who had disconnected his gas supply, and winning £400 compensation in the process.

It is likely that some of these bodies will be familiar to you, especially the Citizens Advice Bureau (CAB) and *Which?*, but they are all useful if you have a particular issue with any of the industries which they monitor. That they do not have direct, legally enforced powers is not necessarily a reason to ignore them. Companies in those sectors are keenly aware that they have a positive public profile, and can therefore attract good media attention, which in turn can put the heat on a chief executive at precisely the wrong time. Being perceived to be on the side of the argument against your customers is never going to work out well.

The regulator will also be interested in what they have to say, not least when it is reviewing its next set of price caps for a particular sector. It is also difficult for a company to attack a trusted body such as CAB, which is greatly respected by the British public, without the company coming off worse. This is why you will need to get these bodies onside if you want an additional authoritative voice to make your case.

Consumer bodies are always keen to be noticed and heard, as they tend to be relatively small organisations and therefore rely on a good run of interesting consumer stories to stay alive. Given their special status as 'super complainants', there is also a pressure on them to justify their status in the eyes of the new government. There is no doubt that some are seen to be more effective than others, and in an age of deregulation, ministers expect to see activity and delivery.

The bodies range in size from the tiny, to big players such as CAB, but for all types there are various ways of contacting them, by telephone, email or traditional letter. The best method is to first telephone Consumer Direct to log your particular issue. You will be given a reference number and the call centre operative will do all they can to advise you of your full consumer rights and provide suggested next steps. The type of case they might receive is an energy customer who has been cut off by their supplier. Most of the time, Consumer Direct will then follow up with the energy company and try to resolve the issue. However, many complaints can be difficult to resolve and Consumer Direct would advise on the most suitable body to take an issue to a higher level. They will put you in touch with the organisation best placed to help.

Given that the CAB is going to become an increasingly important organisation, with beefed up powers, it is worthwhile to engage them as early as possible. On the website you can track down the details of your nearest CAB office. Everyone is offered a short session with an assessor, who will identify the most appropriate way to help.

Depending on your particular needs, they might ask you come back again to discuss your problem further. Alternatively, they might judge that a different organisation that is better placed to help you.

Spending time to talk with Consumer Direct or CAB is often worthwhile, but the only problem with going via this route is that it is akin to joining an orderly queue. You need to be a troublemaker from time to time, as they are the people that companies tend to engage with more quickly.

As I explain in chapter 4, using consumer watchdogs passively, by copying them into a letter or email can be sufficient to make companies nervous. The more clued up you seem, the more of a threat you are. In most instances, where you can find them, it is worth working out the email address of the head of any consumer bodies you wish to contact. You can do this by doing an internet search to ascertain the usual format of an email to that organisation and then using the body's webpage to find out who the leader is.

The fear of politicians

We have already proclaimed MPs to be surprisingly powerful in everyday consumer battles, and if you ask any major CEO or Chairman, they always keep a nervous eye on political interventions. Many CEOs do not have a great natural enthusiasm for politics, being far more interested in specific sectors and competitors than the goings on in Westminster. But they are acutely aware that political decisions, either domestic or in Brussels, can have a direct impact on their careers.

As elected representatives, MPs have the freedom to treat CEOs with an appalling lack of respect, whether hauling them before a select committee and questioning them on their salary, bonus or pension, or placing additional taxes upon their business or sector.

A personal example of how easily companies find themselves getting it wrong was when an MP travelled through Gatwick Airport, accidentally carrying a small knife used for peeling fruit. For some reason, the knife was not detected via the usual security checks. The MP discovered that she had this knife when she was on holiday and was disturbed that it had not been detected. On her return from holiday, she raised the issue at the customer help desk. Two weeks later, she had not even the courtesy of a reply. In the meantime, she no doubt fumed, as MPs do not like to be ignored. Put simply, the team at the airport had panicked and sat on the complaint until it was too late and the problem was now out of control. The poisoned chalice was offered my way so I tried to rescue the situation but the MP had possession of more facts than I had. She told me, within a minute of speaking, that she had decided to raise this security issue in the House of Commons. I tried to talk her down, but even I found it difficult to rebut what had been a complete dropped catch from the airport team. Because she was disappointed with the response, she did go ahead and raised the issue in Parliament (naming me too, in fact). So what should have been a straightforward fix became a public relations balls-up. Why? Because the issue was not dealt with quickly and efficiently. And this illustrates my point throughout this book, namely that people with full possession of the skills and knowledge of the political system are able to take a bad consumer experience and publicly embarrass a company into action. Putting the right pressure on the right people bears fruit so often.

The role of regulators

Although she remains a divisive figure in British politics, former Conservative Prime Minister Margaret Thatcher developed a radical proposal in government, namely to privatise a host of state owned basic services. This included energy companies, water providers, telecommunications, airlines and airports. To be fair to the Conservative administration of the time the companies in question were horrendously inefficient. It took a couple of months to get a phone line connected, and when you did you could have the choice of only one type of telephone.

The water and energy infrastructure was crumbling, starved of investment and beset by decades of trade union interference. The economy lacked dynamism, and the battles of the 1970s had left Britain exhausted and second-rate: a fading post-imperialist power. Water pipes were rotting and power stations still predominantly burned coal.

Thatcher unleashed the forces of the free-market upon these basic services and private money began to pour in, but she could hardly privatise and then allow government to simply walk away from its responsibilities. Even Thatcher realised that if left unattended with complete freedom, the companies would be sorely tempted to ramp up costs without fear of losing customers.

A utility will put forward its recommendations as to the type of improvements it needs to make over a five-year period and then asks the regulator to approve it. Of course, this is a negotiation, and the regulator will often refuse to accede immediately, especially as the customers of that regulated utility will also be strongly arguing for more costs to be absorbed by the company itself. In order to provide a more stable environment for investment and reduce the risks associated with political uncertainty, economic regulation has been carried out independently of government by regulators within a framework of duties enshrined in statute. Significant parts of the UK's infrastructure operate in sectors where there is an element of market power, either natural or 'granted' monopolies. A natural monopoly often occurs because it is simply too expensive for a new market entrant to replicate the infrastructure which already exists. The most obvious examples of natural monopolies are utilities such as gas, electricity and water, at least in terms of distributing the services to customers.

This is especially the case in the water industry. It is a basic service which we all need to live, but water is a difficult thing to move about, and it also has a nasty habit of leaking, getting contaminated or evaporating. So the most efficient way to provide it to people is to store it locally and send it to homes and businesses via pipes. But this means that only one company can provide you with your water. If you live in Maidstone, it is unlikely that United Utilities (based in the north west) can provide you with the water you need, so you have no choice but to use the local provider regardless of their performance.

There is a major upside and a major downside to being a regulated company. On the upside, the level of inherent risk in the business is far lower than in other sectors. This is why, especially at a time when the global economy is volatile, investors choose to put their money into utilities. In recent years we have seen the purchase of several UK regulated companies by foreign investors, such as ScottishPower (now owned by Iberdrola of Spain), Thames Water (led by

Australia's Macquarie Bank), and BAA (Ferrovial, also of Spain). The money they can earn from utilities tends to be lower, but far safer because the regulator ensures a steady return. It could be compared with putting your savings into a building society rather than playing the stock market.

On the downside, regulated companies tend to find it difficult to grow as quickly as companies which are not restricted in this way. If you begin to generate too much income, the regulator will recognise this and provide a smaller rate of return at the time of the next price review. Investment in infrastructure is often capital intensive, long term and with significant sunk costs, i.e. those which have already been incurred and cannot be recovered.

But a regulated company often has little incentive to invest heavily in anything unless there is a guaranteed return. Think back to my Coca-Cola story. Here was a major brand who felt they had to try something new, and so ultimately took a decision which they could not be certain would pay off. It did not, and market forces told the management it needed to return to the original formula as soon as possible or the company would suffer. If you are an energy company or airport, there is no such risk. You agree with the regulator that you can build a new power station or airport terminal, and in return you will get a guaranteed rate of return.

Often this lack of competitive pressure has a detrimental impact on the quality of the service you receive. If you have a complaint, what are you going to do about it? Switch off your water supply and use Evian instead? As you cannot leave your water supplier and go elsewhere, you have to consider other ways to put pressure on them. When they are going through their regulatory review, the water company will submit a plea for a higher rate of return. They will argue that the water infrastructure they inherited when the company was privatised is in need of urgent repair and replacement. If they cannot replace the pipes, there will be more water wasted, a precious natural resource which has become even more important as we head into the expected changes to our climate. So they say give us the money now to invest and it will safeguard consumers in the future. The regulator, unless they are feeling especially generous, will push back and argue that the company itself will need to find ways to run its business more efficiently and do things more cheaply. This could mean cutting back office staff, or simplifying its internal functions such as IT. It requires them to justify the prices they hope to charge for the next five year period. This means that the affected companies only get a brief break from this cycle of regulatory reviews.

Of course, not everyone agrees that this is the best system. For example, most people want their energy bills to be as low as possible. But cutting bills might mean lower investment in measures to tackle climate change, which has become a significant priority for many Western governments. Due to the media's unsophisticated approach to the interlinked relationship between prices and investment, consumers are unsurprisingly also confused.

Regulators are the bane of most relevant companies' lives, forcing them to beg (sometimes unsuccessfully) to increase the costs they can pass to consumers, whilst having to deliver expensive infrastructure improvements at the same time. The regulatory process always creates losers in every review of every sector. Sometimes it is perceived to have unfairly bene- fited the infrastructure or service providers, and sometimes the consumer. Whatever the final outcome of the review, you can be sure that prices will increase to some degree, provok- ing headlines in the *Daily Mail*.

Fortunately, regulated utilities are some of the best companies to unleash your soon-to-be developed lobbying skills upon. Regulated companies are especially susceptible to attacks from its customers during this key period when the regulator is understandably swayed by external events, especially if a company in question is being attacked in Parlia- ment or the media. A bad press during this critical period could literally wipe millions off of its future income, so this is worth bearing in mind when they give you poor customer service. It is unlikely that your single case of a broken boiler or miscalculated energy bill is going to directly impact on a company's financial settlement, but it adds to the impression of a company which is either doing the right thing or the wrong thing by its consumers (who, after all, the regulator should be obsessed with).

For at least a year and a half beforehand, the regulators become an almost obsessive focus for these companies. Each company in these sectors will have a dedicated regulatory team who will be providing endless reams of papers and conduct numerous meetings and phone calls to make their case. But these regulatory teams can only influence the process so far, because if the company becomes publicly vilified for its poor customer service then its attempts to persuade the regulator will fall flat. The job of the utility company is to minimise the reasons for getting a bad deal. Any adverse publicity can only harm their cause, so the company becomes especially risk-averse. This is good news for you as they are far more likely to respond positively to your demands for a refund and/or an apology.

How to contact a CEO

Contacting a chief executive of a FTSE-100 company is not going to be easy – in fact it is infinitely more difficult to get to them than a senior MP. This is explained by the fact that politicians are elected and paid for by us, therefore they are directly accountable to us. CEOs are not. The likelihood of a senior business leader answering their own calls is as remote as Fiji winning the World Cup. Instead they have a human filter system in place which will send callers to the relevant person or department in the company. A media enquiry goes to the communication team; an irate customer gets packed off to the customer services team, etc.

On this basis I would not bother attempting to reach a business leader by telephone as it will be doomed to fail. If you do, expect to encounter a sharp response. The idea that you have had the temerity to contact someone so important will annoy their PAs or general assistants far more than the CEOs themselves. I refer to it as the Armani factor. If you go shopping in designer clothes shop and are not dripping with diamonds or already dressed in Armani, you are often treated with scant regard. Not by the brand itself, or whoever owns the actual retail outlet, but usually by the shop assistants, who are poorly paid and almost certainly could not afford to buy the clothes for themselves. They adopt a protective attitude towards the exclusivity of what they represent, and want you to understand that they are different, better, than their counterparts in Next or Topshop. CEOs can sometimes have similar people working for them – they take their roles as gatekeepers to extremes and can be quite unfriendly. However, even in the face of bad manners and provocation, you are always advised to keep your cool. The more reasonable your tone of voice (as well as the words you use), the more difficult it is for people to fob you off and deny you access.

Given that telephone is not likely to be fruitful, you are best advised to send an email. Most senior people will have a handheld device such as a BlackBerry or iPad with which they can keep up to date with their latest messages. Although they will not sit around reading every message which is directed to them, there will be certain times of the day or occasions when it might just make it through the barrier. That is why an early morning email (before 8.30-9.00hrs is best) can be effective as the corporate leader can see it as they are being driven to the office. Reading an email from a customer who is eloquent with a balanced and measured threat, will irritate the boss and can lead to action.

You can, of course, send a letter but it will be treated simi-larly to a telephone call, by giving the PA time to consider who best to farm the answer out to. It is unlikely that the CEO will even see the content of the letter, and the PA might even sign it in his or her absence. There will also be a standard response to a whole range of enquiries – template paragraphs covering a whole range of eventualities, designed to damn you with blandness.

In order to track down the relevant information, you will need to visit the website of the company and go to the 'contacts' section. This will at least give you the central telephone number and postal address for the company. You may also get the name of the chief executive. But be warned: it is not always clear in a big international retailer with a parent company who the chief executive is. For example, a UK FTSE-100 company such as Kingfisher plc does not own any stores or products named 'Kingfisher'; instead it is comprised of DIY favourites such as B&Q and Screwfix. Both Kingfisher and B&Q have separate leaders, so you have to be sure who you are trying to target in that instance. This is also the same for companies such as Proctor and Gamble which have over 300 separate products under their ownership, such as Head & Shoulders shampoo, and Max Factor make-up.

Once you have worked out who you are writing to, you need to track down the email address for the chief executive. Email addresses are far more difficult to track down but a group of consumers have banded together and created a simple but ingenious website named CEO Email, which has a huge list of major corporations and the email addresses for the chief executive for each instance. Some may fall out of date (not least because the CEOs might have them changed due to the emergence of the site), but the tables of names also includes the date when the accuracy of the address was last checked. It is worth repeating that targeting the CEO remains the last, not the first, step in the process.

When you are contacting a company you should aim for 100 per cent victory, but at the same time have in your mind how you will feel if you get slightly less. I am a firm believer that you must stand firm to being fobbed off, but I also try to remain realistic. In the case of getting a refund, nothing but the full amount should be enough. But in some circumstances you might be content with receiving vouchers for the same amount. You might also decide that the principle of a given issue is more important than simply getting a refund. Make sure you have a legitimate case before you embark too far down this route. You know when you are in the right because you find yourself seething with anger at the injustice. Keep your powder dry until you need it to explode.

Chapter 3: Lobbying

What is lobbying?

The generally accepted definition of the term 'lobbying' is the influencing of legislators and officials in the government by individuals, other legislators, constituents, or advocacy groups. A lobbyist is a person who tries to influence decisions on legislation on behalf of a special interest, or someone who is a member of a lobby group.

This is all fairly straightforward but I use the term lobbying not as a special practice carried out by well-paid public relations types, but actually as something every one of us does already. Whether you are arguing for the construction of a new nuclear power station or whether you are trying to get someone to join your local community group, in both instances you are trying to persuade a decision-maker. Children lobby their parents when they angle for a new toy. They work out which parent is the softest touch, and then try to persuade them with whatever method works best – tantrums, guilt or love. When we try to get a promotion or a pay rise at work, we are engaged in a form of lobbying.

Lobbying might be direct face-to-face contact or involve a fully mapped out campaign strategy. A charity looking to increase awareness of a Third World issue (such as increasing state aid to Africa, for example) is lobbying. An energy company trying to persuade government to build a coal-fired power station is also lobbying. But these inherent skills are not as frequently used in consumer or community situations, perhaps because we now see lobbying as something practised by experts or hired hands. I strongly believe that the time is right to acknowledge that lobbying is a natural and often helpful practice, which can be a genuine force for good.

The term itself shouldn't be attacked – it's what you are doing it for that really counts. What could be better than learning how to lobby for yourself, for your family and your community? Politicians, partly wishing to distract attention from their own foibles, love to scrutinise and anguish over it. But I believe it is time for the term to be reclaimed from the critics and conspiracy theorists, because lobbying is not something we should be ashamed exists.

In its twenty or so years, lobbying in the UK has grown from a slightly murky activity practised by a few well-placed Westminster operators to a full-blown multimillion pound industry. There are tons of firms which specialise in providing advice to corporate interests, councils and even charities such as Oxfam. The industry has its own trade associations, with codes of conduct in place. Occasionally, lobbying gets embroiled in controversy, but most of the time you will have heard little about it.

In short, lobbying can bring important issues to the attention of policymakers and regulators, who would otherwise inadvertently make bad law. It may appear that subsidising renewable energy is a great idea and should be rushed through Parliament at breakneck speed, but unless industry and other interested parties respond there can be no 'sense check' about the policy's unintended consequences.

But lobbying is also a two-way process. By engaging with industry, business leaders and citizens, politicians can improve their own understanding of complex issues. Those who campaign against lobbying always appear to have a very dim view of the ability of policymakers to come to decisions without somehow having been inappropriately persuaded by a special interest. So if a minister decides that he or she wants to build a new runway, then it must be because the aviation industry or big business has forced or seduced them into doing so, and not because they have arrived at a view based on consideration of the full pros and cons.

But with freedom also comes responsibility, and lobbying should always be undertaken in a clear, transparent and ethical way. This ensures that people have faith in the process of public advocacy and its relationship with democratic institutions such as Parliament. A small number of high-profile lobbying scandals have ensured that measures have been put in place to self-regulate the industry in order to ensure accountability if and when lobbyists get it wrong.

If you need an example of what the world would be like with a ban on the lobbying of policymakers and politicians, just consider what would fill its place. Consultations have been en vogue for many years now, but how often do you believe that they change anything? If a mobile phone company launched a consultation about a planned mast to be positioned on your road, would your involvement in this official process make a jot of difference? Consultations have their place, of course, but not if they are simply to be a box-ticking exercise for a company or government which has already reached its conclusions before it has begun. Lobbying is different because it motivates communities and individuals to respond and therefore offers a better chance of change.

Most campaigns are carefully drawn up on the basis of what effectively constitutes 'enlightened self-interest' for any given person or company. For example, the nuclear industry might ask government for a special tax break to incentivise the building of new power stations. In one sense, this is naked opportunism by the industry – the bigger the subsidy, the lower the risk, and the greater sums of money it is possible to make. However, it could also be argued that the government's subsidy has a benefit to the rest of us too – nuclear produces very little carbon dioxide, so climate change emissions can be significantly cut. Everyone is a winner. Well almost, because the renewable energy sector would also argue that they should receive an even bigger subsidy given that their technologies have even less impact on the environment. Nuclear is better placed, partly because its lobbyists are better positioned to make the case to the decision-makers in government, and it is better funded.

However, money is not everything in lobbying (thank goodness, you say) because UK politics and the media love an underdog. A local campaign group can easily outmanoeuvre a global juggernaut because it has a human face and is much more difficult to say 'no' to.

A brief history of lobbying

Lobbying has been around for as long as politics itself, and is a legitimate part of the democratic system. Those who wish all lobbying could be outlawed should remember that there are countries where that is the case and they are not especially healthy examples of modern democracies (see North Korea, Burma and Turkmenistan).

But the ability of individuals or organisations to put forward their case as to why they deserve consideration from policymakers is crucially important to maintaining good public policy outcomes. In the UK it has always been a legal activity, dating back to the signing of Britain's most important legal framework: the Magna Carta signed by King John in 1215. The document provides the 'right to petition the government for the redress of grievances'. The right to lobby is also covered by the First Amendment to the United States' Constitution, where it prevents attempts to prohibit the 'petitioning for a government redress of grievances'.

Professional lobbying in the UK has been in existence since the 1930s but first gained a significant foothold in the late 1970s and early 1980s, and at that time it was a new frontier, with few rules. Interestingly, some of the early players in UK lobbying actually encouraged moves towards regulation of the industry. However, the regulations failed to come into force.

With the benefit of hindsight this lack of clear rules was always likely to end badly. Three major scandals have erupted over the past couple of decades, and each has tarnished the lobbying industry. The first played a role in bringing down John Major's Conservative government of the mid 1990s; the second was the first major scandal to hit Tony Blair's new Labour; the last came most recently when former ministers attempted to offer their services to big business upon retirement from Parliament. Given that you might only have a vague understanding of what happened in each instance, let us take a brief look at each scandal and their consequences.

The Cash for Questions scandal erupted when a Westminster lobbying company was exposed as having paid tens of thousands of pounds to two high-flying Conservative MPs, in exchange for asking parliamentary questions at £2,000 a time on behalf of Harrods.

Neil Hamilton, at that stage a minister responsible for business probity, and Tim Smith, a junior Northern Ireland minister, were named in 1994 as recipients of payments passed to Ian Greer Associates by Mohamed Al Fayed, the owner of Harrods, on top of a £50,000 fee for a parliamentary lobbying campaign.

The payments made by Al Fayed were sent in a two-year period when the government was investigating his takeover of House of Fraser, including Harrods. Al Fayed said that he had been approached by the lobbyist Ian Greer who offered to run a campaign on his behalf. At the time, Al Fayed was facing considerable criticism from a number of Conservative MPs. He was told by Greer that aside from the project fee payable to Greer himself, any parliamentary questions would cost extra, with the money sent directly to Hamilton and Smith. The most famous remark from this whole sorry episode was when Greer allegedly said to Al Fayed: 'You need to rent an MP just like you rent a taxi.'

Tim Smith admitted taking money from Al Fayed and resigned immediately from his junior ministerial role. However, both Hamilton and Greer denied the charges and took immediate legal action, which was finally dropped in 1996. Greer's lobbying firm collapsed and although Hamilton continued to defy his party leader and stood again in the safe Tory seat of Tatton, his political career was brought swiftly to an end. It eventually led to the circus of the 1997 general election battle when former BBC journalist Martin Bell defeated him in a landslide victory.

This saga left a stain which tainted the Conservative Party and lobbying for many years. There is a certain irony that 'paid for' questions were rightly outlawed, but 'asked for' questions still frequently occur. A body can still approach a Member of Parliament and ask whether they will consider tabling a question on their behalf. Many MPs are relatively relaxed about such activities, as long as money is not changing hands.

When Tony Blair swept into Downing Street with his record breaking majority in 1997, it seemed that the sleaze of the Tory government had gone with it. But sleaze does not stay attached to just one party for very long. New Labour had been enthusiastically received by the public, but to the corporate world it was still an unknown quantity, which meant that previously ignored MPs, policy wonks and left-leaning lobbyists were in great demand. Inevitably perhaps, this led to people getting carried away by the sudden attention and opportunities to make serious money.

In 1998 an investigative journalist called Greg Palast produced a story, published in *The Observer*, detailing evidence that former Labour Party advisers to Cabinet members and even the Prime Minister had influenced policies in return for a fee. *The Observer* study is the most comprehensive exposé on 'special access' to ministers ever produced, before or since.[6]

---

6. The full report can be found at www.gregpalast.com/lobbygate-there-are-17-people-that-count-to-say-that-i-am-intimate-with-every-one-of-them-is-the-under-statement-of-the-century/

The Observer explained how and when and to whom they made the fixes. Palast got a tip that lobbying firms close to Blair's New Labour government were getting their hands on inside information which they were passing on to their clients.

The key figure in the investigation was the colourful New Labour 'fixer', and former researcher to Peter Mandelson, Derek Draper. He had happily told the investigative team of his special access to the Treasury and 10 Downing Street. He boasted that he had secured a senior business leader a place on a government task force. In his most famous quote, Draper told Palast: 'There are seventeen people who count, and to say I am intimate with every one of them is the understatement of the century.' He went on to claim that he had got Jonathan Powell, the Prime Minister's then chief of staff and gatekeeper at No. 10, his job.

Draper, continuing to show off, apparently stood up at the same meeting and read a series of phone messages from his pager. The names included the now Labour leader Ed Miliband, his brother David and even Ed Balls, then Gordon Brown's trusted adviser at the Treasury. 'I don't want to be a consultant,' he said. 'I just want to stuff my bank account at £250 an hour.'

At one point, Draper had told the reporter, 'I think there will be a scandal here eventually. The curtain is going to come down. I'm sure it will happen.' He was right. For two weeks, every paper in Britain ran nothing but 'lobbygate' stories on their front pages. When the story broke, Draper lost his job and ministers disassociated themselves from him. He disappeared from the political scene until Gordon Brown brought him back in ten years later.

A new 'access' scandal emerged in the dying days of Gordon Brown's tenure as Prime Minister, which led to three former ministers being suspended from the Parliamentary Labour Party. Stephen Byers, Geoff Hoon and Patricia Hewitt had all been members of the Cabinet at various times but were recorded by an undercover reporter promising to provide introductions in return for money once they had stood down as MPs.

The allegations arose from a *Dispatches/Sunday Times* investigation, screened by Channel 4, in which Byers, Hoon and Hewitt were amongst six parliamentarians secretly filmed discussing the possibility of working for what they thought was an American lobby company.

Byers told the reporter that he was a 'cab for hire' for up to £5,000 a day, whilst Ms Hewitt, a former health secretary, recommended paying a think-tank to sit next to a minister at dinner. Hoon, a former defence secretary, pitched his fees at £3,000 a day.

In none of these instances could it be proved that they influenced government policy, but for the public the impression was extremely poor, especially so soon after the expenses scandal. Even their own side was quick to attack them publicly, with Mandelson suggesting that, 'It is extremely disappointing, and it is very sad and rather grubby.' The government investigated, concluded that nothing illegal had taken place and the matter was lost in the sound and fury of the general election campaign.

Lobbying is often perceived as deals being made behind closed doors, and thanks in part to these three monumental scandals this impression has been reinforced, as usually the politician or lobbyist is snared by grainy hidden camera footage. Of course, the reality of almost any workplace is that meetings take place in private, so it is hardly a surprise that a minister would meet with a company or pressure group behind closed doors.

There is also a widely-held view that big companies can buy influence by hiring the right people to represent them, especially if those people have recently worked in government. In reality, even the most powerful business leaders do not have the ability to change the direction of the government by simply what they say (and thank goodness for that).

Of course, they do influence outcomes because they are respected voices in the business community, and their weight ensures that the media takes notice too. Media coverage is then another form of influence on decision-makers. But a meeting behind closed doors of a businessman demanding and getting a minister to change his or her mind simply does not happen.

The unfortunate thing about the coverage of these three particular lobbying or access scandals is they are amongst the few times the public will have been made aware of what the industry does. Rather than provide an accurate picture of lobbying, they provide a distorted view. This then feeds into the political response, which tends to be based on suspicion and fear. The result is a pressure on policymakers to 'do some-thing' about the industry, which in response has become more professionalised.

Professional lobbying

The professionalisation of lobbying has partly taken place because of a need to better self-regulate the industry, but primarily it is because it has become a proper, recognised vocation which requires skills and knowledge. It began as a side earner for existing politicians who discovered that they could trade access to ministers in return for money. But now it is much more professional, with consultants whose value is less about connections and more about the ability to create smart campaigns, shaping and helping to deliver strong argu-ments in a public policy debate.

Professional lobbying tends to be any activity which is designed to influence the actions or decisions of the institu-tions of government. 'Government relations' tends to do exactly what it says on the tin, namely direct contact with those decision-making institutions; 'public affairs' (lobbying) is also concerned with engaging those groups which indirectly influence policy such as the media, grass roots organisations, NGOs (e.g. green groups) or think-tanks.

Lobbyists can be found everywhere, not just in the dining rooms of Parliament. They can include:

- Public Affairs Consultancies: provide political advocacy in return for a fee, usually to large companies.
- Law Firms/Management Consultancies: as above, but usually with a more specialist edge.
- NGOs: these includes organisations that campaign for particular policy outcomes such as protection of the environment, in the case of Greenpeace and Friends of the Earth.
- Think-tanks: they do not tend to lobby in return for a fee, but they try to influence the public policy debate through conferences and written papers.
- Trade Associations: most major sectors will have a trade body which represents their general interests. For example, the house builder Barrett's will talk to politicians and regulators as an individual company but also use the Home Builders Federation for much of its lobbying effort.
- Public Relations Consultancies: some agencies do not have a designated public affairs service, but can still lobby on behalf of clients by influencing media and editorial opinion. However most PR companies now have a public affairs service within them.
- Companies/In-House Representatives: almost every company in the FTSE-100 will have a person, or persons, responsible for overseeing and managing that company's political relations. But they often also use an external agency to assist, both with strategy and day-to-day research and admin.
- Pressure Groups and Individuals: these groups are becoming increasingly common as the internet provides new opportunities for people to rally behind a particular single cause. Some individuals also lobby, but this is relatively rare as people motivated to campaign on an issue will usually join with others to do so.

- Trade Unions: unions lobby government and business organisations for better pay, working conditions and health and safety.
- Journalists: most journalists are simply a 'medium' between the news and the viewer/listener, but some take a special interest in an issue and start a campaign aimed at changing public policy. Examples include John Pilger, who has devoted much of his career to criticising US foreign policy; Mark Dowie, who published an investigation of the dangers in the Ford Pinto car; and going back even further, the investigation of William Thomas Stead into child prostitution in Victorian London, which led to the Criminal Law Amendment Act of 1885.

Companies employ people to lobby on their behalf for all sorts of reasons, but not because they believe the political system can be circumnavigated by old school tie contacts or used banknotes in brown paper envelopes. They employ experts because they can help companies to understand how to approach any given politician or legislative process. The complaint often made about professional lobbying is that it is too centred on the 'whom' rather than the 'what', with close contacts with decision-makers the key selling point. That is not the reality. Knowing important and influential politicians is useful, but primarily because it is easier to then guess what they are likely to do or say on a given topic.

Where next for lobbying?

The Association of Professional Political Consultants (APPC) is the representative and self-regulating body for the industry. Its main role is to ensure transparency and openness of members' lobbying activities via an agreed code of conduct. It has done a good job of helping to promote the much greater transparency in the industry, but the leash of tighter regulation is still being threatened.

In 2009 the House of Commons Public Administration

Select Committee recommended that a statutory register of lobbying activity and lobbyists would improve transparency of the dealings between Whitehall decision-makers and outside interests. Parliament responded to this recommendation by saying that self-regulation was more practical. The Prime Minister David Cameron, when in opposition, predicted that lobbying was 'the next big scandal waiting to happen' and was one that had 'tainted our politics for too long, an issue that exposes the far-too-cosy relationship between politics, government, business and money'. He promised a Conservative government would stop the lobbying industry's attempts through former ministers to access and influence policy.

The Conservative leader said that the '£2 billion industry' has a big presence at Westminster and in some cases MPs are approached more than 100 times a week by lobbyists. He said he wanted to shine 'the light of transparency' on lobbying so that politics 'comes clean about who is buying power and influence'.

Organisations such as the Alliance for Lobbying Transparency have welcomed Cameron's rhetoric that something needs to be done about lobbying. But they are calling for much stronger measures such as a mandatory register of lobbyists so the public 'can see who is lobbying whom, and the extent to which national policies are being influenced by commercial forces'.[7]

This has progressed further following the 2010 general election when the new Conservative–Liberal Democrat coalition pledged, 'The parties will tackle lobbying through introducing a statutory register of lobbyists.' This process will take some time to resolve itself, but a decision is likely at some point in 2012.

Lobbying today is a busy, sometimes lucrative but ever changing industry. But parliamentary lobbying has become less of a feature. Why? The sad truth is that the UK Parliament has diminished in stature over the past few decades with the

---

7. http://www.telegraph.co.uk/news/election-2010/7189466/David-Cameron-warns-lobbying-is-next-political-scandal.html

emergence of devolved government in Scotland, Wales and Northern Ireland, as well as the rise in powers of the European Union. There has also been a fundamental change in the actual role of the two chambers of the House of Commons and the Lords, with fewer and fewer major announcements being made from the despatch box, and many more being 'leaked' to the national press. In a technique commonly referred to as 'kite-flying', a government will allow a proposed tax increase or new initiative on law and order to be briefed to a political editor. If the public reaction the following morning is good, then the policy measure can be introduced; if not, it will be ditched amid denials that it was ever being considered at all. This may be good politics, but it is bad democracy.

How to lobby
To be a successful lobbyist, you must first get to grip with the basics. My key tips, with thanks to industry stalwart Robbie McDuff, are as follows:

> ›   Do your research: understand the needs/pressures on the person(s) who is taking the final decision on a given policy.

> ›   Understand the system: if you are working to help amend legislation, which is making its way through a departmental consultation or the House of Commons, you need to know the actual mechanics of how a Bill or review is likely to progress. There is no point making a case for a proposal after the deadline has passed.

> ›   Work with the flow of policy (where at all possible): it is pointless trying to get the government (or other body) to do something which you know they have absolutely no intention of doing. This is why it is important to try to get policymakers to accommodate a change rather than force them to entirely U-turn, which is extremely difficult to do.

› Get in early: the best time to involve yourself in a public policy decision is when the discussion has first begun. It tends to be the early feedback from interested parties that governments listen to, rather than at the end of the process.

› Don't rely on knowing people, but do find out who the right people are: regardless of the boasting and bragging of Derek Draper and Stephen Byers, governments do not change their minds because individuals call them up and ask them to. You should never rely on personal relationships to provide a shortcut to presenting a properly thought-out campaign. However, it is important to know who the key decision-makers are, so you can then tailor your campaign message to persuade them of your case.

› Develop support in peacetime: as I suggested in the chapter on politicians, you should try to engage your local MP when you do not have anything specific to ask of them. Politicians get hundreds of requests a day, all asking them to prioritise a particular issue. When you build relationships in time of calm, you are more likely to be listened to in times of turmoil.

› Use communications aids: where possible this can really strengthen your case. It is good practice to distil your arguments into a one- or two-page document which you can then share with busy politicians and other decision-makers. If they forget what you were discussing, they can at least have a summary to refer to at a later date.

› Try to operate below the radar until you are pushed overground: it is always better to try to work with governments and other decision-makers before you feel the need to publicly attack. Once you press that button you risk alienating your targets, and then your campaign will be lost. Sometimes, of course, campaigns do need to go public in order to win.

› Identify champions for the cause: almost every campaign has at least someone who supports it. Identifying your advocates and then ensuring you keep them informed is vital to the success or otherwise of your campaign.

› Assess both sides: it is a useful exercise to assess the strength of the arguments which may be used against you as well as the ones in favour. Once you have identified those that will be used by the opposition, you can then begin to address them.

Case study: The Gurkhas and Joanna Lumley

One of the great and best known examples of a successful lobbying campaign was spearheaded by television and film star Joanna Lumley on behalf of the Gurkha veterans. Until 2004 Gurkhas were not allowed to settle in the UK. Tony Blair's Labour government changed the rules and allowed Gurkhas to settle if they had retired after 1997 (when the brigade HQ moved from Hong Kong to Britain), but older veterans were denied the same rights except in exceptional circumstances. The courts eventually ruled that this policy was illegal because of the arbitrary nature of the cut-off point. In turn the government agreed to produce new rules, but these still denied the veterans an automatic right to settle in the UK.

The complaint from the campaign was that people who had fought for this country for more than 200 years, with over 50,000 dying in service, should also have the right to settle here. The counter argument from the government was that the potential cost of the many thousands of veterans coming over to the UK could be huge, costing the UK taxpayer as much as £1.4 billion.

Governments have to make difficult choices with public expenditure on a daily basis, but most are hidden and not nearly as emotive as the Gurkha issue became. The combined force of Conservatives, Liberal Democrats and rebel Labour MPs managed to inflict an embarrassing defeat upon the government, and pass a motion which would allow Gurkhas who served before 1997 residence in the UK.

However, on 6 May 2009, just a day after meeting with the Prime Minister, Lumley discovered that another five veterans has had their applications turned down. The minister for immigration, Phil Woolas (later ejected from Parliament for inappropriate election literature), was facing questions from the BBC News channel when it became apparent that Lumley and the rest of the Gurkha campaign were just outside of the studio. The moment the minister walked out of the room he was 'doorstepped' and a hastily arranged meeting took place. Woolas argued that although the veterans' applications had been technically rejected, the final paragraph of the letters actually provided a glimmer of light in suggesting that they could be reassessed in the coming months. In truth the government was in a complete tail spin, and hoping they could get through the day by showing just enough leg to satisfy the campaigners but not committing the government to a full U-turn.

Most campaigners will have considered a meeting with the minister a day's job well done but Lumley did what all great lobbyists do, namely strike whilst the iron is hot. Recognising that Woolas was rattled and seeing his career flash before his eyes, Lumley got him to agree to join her for an impromptu press conference in front of a curious media. She gave an extremely positive spin on the minister's comments, pointedly staring at him until he nodded his head in agreement. It was the equivalent of a political mugging. The footage of the minister looking ashen-faced is a classic of its type (and still available on YouTube[8]). He knew she was misrepresenting the meeting but to suddenly start a public fight with a national treasure before the world's

---

8. http://www.youtube.com/watch?v=BcdeK27Y65s

media would have been political suicide. So he sat there and took it, with the day ending with Lumley's arms held aloft outside of Parliament surrounded by the veterans.

Why did it work? Let's take a moment to pick out the key themes which made the campaign such a success:

› A good cause: defending the rights of people who had fought for Britain in war is a noble campaign, and this immediately makes the process of influencing government much easier.

› Clear campaign aims: unlike a whole host of public policy campaigns which are difficult to explain in one minute on someone's doorstep, the rights of Gurkha veterans to settle in Britain was clear.

› Catchy slogans and sound bites: the visuals of Lumley holding aloft a Kukri sword, surrounded by veterans in wheelchairs and with walking sticks was burned into the memory of every decision-maker and was ideal for both television and newspapers.

› A well-organised team: although everyone remembers Lumley as the driver of the campaign, in reality the hard work was undertaken by behind-the-scenes staffers who deserve as much credit as she does.

› Prominent and popular spokesperson: Lumley is a fully-fledged, undisputed 'national treasure' and putting her at the front of the campaign was a masterstroke.

› Momentum: the campaign did not allow the issue to drop and seizing the moment by grabbing poor Phil Woolas from the confines of the TV studios and parading him before the TV cameras was a great example of how to maintain and accelerate momentum.

› Hard work: above all, the campaign team worked solidly for many months to secure victory. Sweat and tears will always give a campaign that extra advantage.

Of course, the nature of a campaign changes depending on what you are trying to achieve. Joanna Lumley had a personal connection with the veterans as her father served in the 6ᵗʰ Gurkha Rifles, but it's unlikely that she would have put her name to just any campaign. The easiest campaigns to recruit for are ones which have an emotive element to them, such as this one, Oscar-winning actress Emma Thompson opposing the third runway at Heathrow and former Bond-girl Honor Blackman as the voice of the Equitable Life pensioners.

But of the list above, you can still maximise the effectiveness of your campaign regardless of whether you have struck an emotive issue. The government did not lose to Lumley merely because it was on the wrong side of the issue (although it was in terms of public opinion); it failed to nail the reasons why the rules were as they were; it failed to get a grip on errant backbenchers; it used Phil Woolas, an unimpressive and grey spokesman, as the public face of the government; and when faced with certain defeat, it failed to give in gracefully and in a timely manner to at least get some credit for having done so.

Lumley's campaign was also extremely successful at winning support from other party political interests, with both David Cameron and Nick Clegg taking part in a celebratory press stunt outside of the House of Commons following the victory in the parliamentary vote. Of course, they felt that supporting the Gurkhas was the right thing to do, but they also knew that being associated with Lumley would have positive consequences for them too with the general election less than a year away.

David vs Goliath

To use an example from my personal experience, the collection of campaigners against the previous government's proposed third runway at Heathrow Airport managed to persuade the then shadow transport secretary Theresa Villiers MP to support their cause. Given the strategic importance of the airport to London and the wider UK, it was a big decision to take, but opposing it offered a huge opportunity to say something about what the modern, Cameron-led Conservatives stood for. In many ways, despite the size of the company which owns the airport, the small local campaign group had much better access to Villiers than the aviation industry. Over time they convinced her that they would bitterly oppose any further flights to and from the airport, with the obvious conclusion that a Conservative government would also receive the same treatment.

What the airport campaigners also did well was to play the long game, namely to write off the chances of convincing the government in place to change policy, and instead focus and target the opposition parties who were much more likely to agree to support them. And this was combined with a relentless day-to-day focus on the core aim, namely to prevent any further airport expansion in the UK. Mimicking this refusal to give up in the face of unfavourable odds will impress upon your targets just how strongly you feel about the issue.

What both the anti-Heathrow and Gurkha campaigners realised is that the campaign could not simply rely on a 'Dad's Army' of volunteers offering an hour here or there. Instead they needed a full-time campaign manager who could maintain message discipline. If you are campaigning in the community, you may not be able to afford to offer either the money or time to have a full-time campaign manager, but you can at least identify who will spearhead it as a spokesperson.

The new 'retail' politics means that other politicians will think and act like Theresa Villiers did in the Heathrow example, even in government. There will be more support for David over Goliath over a whole range of issues as the level of trust in big corporations and political institutions continues to diminish. Added to this, 'citizen campaigning' is becoming more professional and better informed, making innovative uses of modern communication techniques.

But there is a downside to any government simply embracing the populist line on any given issue, because it simply doesn't make for good government. It is not that protecting the rights of Gurkha veterans and their families was not the right thing to do, but presumably some other group in society was impacted given that the exchequer only has a finite budget. This may also apply to the Conservative government when they cancelled the policy of airport expansion, because their alternative proposal, namely carving a huge high speed rail line through the politically and environmentally sensitive environs of the Chilterns, will have its own considerable opposition.

Before we start looking at individual campaigns, one of the reasons why powerful companies succeed in getting government to amend policy in their favour is because they ask. Obvious, isn't it? They present a case to policymakers, explain why a particular measure might be detrimental to their sector, usually backing up their case up with hard evidence and analysis. People sometimes complain how unfair it is that such companies get priority, but with all forms of lobbying you get back what you put in. As an individual or as a community campaigner you are also in a position to ask for things to change, or for justice in a particular battle you are fighting. You are probably just one well prepared request away from having your local MP, or even a national spokesman, on your side.

Chapter 4: Campaigning as an individual

Don't get mad, get even

Dave Carroll was a struggling Canadian musician travelling on a United Airlines flight between Halifax and Omaha, with a brief stop in Chicago, in 2008. Having landed in the Windy City, Carroll and his band mates (known as the Sons of Maxwell) were horrified to discover that baggage handlers were literally throwing their instruments onto the tarmac. They tried to alert members of the cabin crew but were given short shrift. When they arrived at their final destination, the band discovered that many of their instruments were broken, including Carroll's beloved 710 Taylor guitar (worth $3,500). United Airlines failed to acknowledge the damage they had caused, and after nine months of jumping through hoops the company finally told him to go away without any offer of compensation.

In his own words Carroll explains what he did next:

> At that moment it occurred to me that I had been fighting a losing battle all this time and that fighting over this at all was a waste of time. The system is designed to frustrate affected customers into giving up their claims and United is very good at it but I realised then that as a songwriter and traveling musician I was not without options. In my final reply to Ms Irlweg [the customer services director] I told her that I would be writing three songs about United Airlines and my experience in the whole matter. I

would then make videos for these songs and offer them for free download on YouTube and my own website, inviting viewers to vote on their favourite United song. My goal: to get one million hits in one year. [9]

Getting one million downloads in one year for his song 'United Breaks Guitars' was a preposterous ambition, and so it proved. In fact, he reached his download target in a matter of days. It is believed that just four days after posting the video online, the share price of United Airlines had crashed by 10 per cent, wiping (on paper at least) $180 million off its value.

The airline had taken a very stupid gamble. They presumed that a standard passenger who flew infrequently with them was of little economic significance. If they could just string him along for enough time, he would eventually give up complaining. They even rejected Carroll's final request, just before the song was released, of just $1,200 in compensation which was less than half of the value of the guitar.

Of course, Carroll had a special talent, namely an ability to write and perform music, but the principle of what he did can be mimicked by anyone. Faced with such appalling customer service, many of us would have just got angry and sent an abusive message out of sheer frustration. How successful would he have been if he had taken the route suggested by the company itself, namely writing letters or emails? How painful would it have been to the airline if Carroll and his friends and family had decided to punish it by simply boycotting United? He chose the smart way, to publicly humiliate the company, which not only gave him a moral victory but meant that he eventually made his money back many times over. You will be pleased to know that Carroll still performs music but he also splits his time as a public speaker on customer relations. Put simply, he turned a negative experience to his advantage.

9. http://www.davecarrollmusic.com/ubg/song1/

How to make a complaint

If you are informed about your rights as a consumer and as a citizen you can get a good deal, but not everyone is, and that is what this book aims to change. Although Dave Carroll's battle with United Airlines ended extremely well for him, the first nine months of complaining got nowhere. That can partly be explained by the fact he got stuck with the wrong person, at the wrong level. The most difficult people to make progress with are mid-level apparatchiks in any organisation, as they usually do not have the power to grant you what you want. In fact, they will often be frowned upon by their superiors if they have given in too easily to a customer demand. The principle of the customer always being right has long been sacrificed.

If you are making a complaint to a company, make sure that you target as high as you can, and involve relevant politicians. Few things put the fear of God into a senior executive more than the thought that his or her company could find itself the target of an aggressive political intervention.

When you get round to crafting your email or letter of complaint, take your time. When you start complaining, make sure you keep a record of telephone calls, letters and emails you send, and if it is a long-term problem (such as a building fault with your new home), then keep a diary or log of the issues you are experiencing. Try to keep a file of replies you get too, even if they have been received by email. Just print them off and put them into a special ring binder.

Do your research. Find out the name and contact details of the chief executive of the company you are targeting. Of course, even when you do get the email address, the direct message to the chief executive is not always the solution because their secretary or personal assistant will often intercept it, possibly forwarding it on to someone else in the company to handle. The way to avoid this is to copy a variety of very important people into the email. To the average secretary panic will ensue because she will know that it is unusual for an email or letter of complaint to be copied to important people, and therefore she cannot avoid showing it to the boss. If you are sending a letter, it is obviously more difficult to get directly to the top man or woman, but writing 'PRIVATE and CONFIDENTIAL' at the top of the envelope will give you a fighting chance. Some CEOs will happily allow their staff to open all letters addressed to them, but others take the request for confidentiality more seriously. If you are telephoning, try to avoid the peak hours of the day, normally from 9am–11am, and 2pm–4pm. When you do get to speak to somebody, always ask for their name, employee code or just a customer reference number. Many calls are recorded, so the operative is unlikely to lie.

In lobbying, like so many other areas of life, clear communication is a fundamental skill. Many people happily abandon the world of essays, papers and dissertations and with it the ability to craft a clear letter of complaint and marshal coherent arguments within it. One benefit of the rise of social networking sites such as Facebook and Twitter, or even the established practice of mobile phone texting, is that people are now trained to be succinct and clear in very few words. But it is also having the effect of losing the art of persuasion, which requires more than the 140 characters offered by Twitter. The most effective letters and emails I have seen always begin with an explanation of the problem, and the development of a logical argument, i.e. a disappointing experience has been had, which has led to my feelings towards the company to change, and can only be resolved if the company intervenes to provide an apology and/or compensation.

The key is to stick to the facts and know your rights when you are asserting them. Do not get bogged down in petty arguments and sideshows/distractions. Once, I found myself fighting for my youngest son's nursery to remain in a hall owned by a local church. The behaviour of the church authorities was extremely bizarre and unreasonable. The lady who ran the nursery had been on the same site for nearly forty years, yet was being treated like a criminal. When I emailed the person in question to ask for the reasons why the established, successful nursery was being threatened with the axe, I started to get ridiculous demands such as the last five years' worth of company accounts before he would even respond to me (this was all clearly a delaying tactic on his part). My strategy was to keep focused on the end goal, namely to put the required pressure on the authorities, but in such a reasonable way that their behaviour seemed entirely unreasonable by comparison. It had the desired effect in that it limited the ammunition available to my opponent.

The simple things to remember about complaining is always to direct your dissatisfaction to the company or organisation first. I know that sounds obvious, but many consumers simply expect not to win, so will immediately head off to an advisory body. That same body is likely to offer the same advice, namely that they cannot help you unless you have tried to help yourself first.

Let us imagine for a moment that, just like Dave Carroll, you have had a bad experience with an airline, named Acme Air for the purposes of this letter. You arrive at the airport in plenty of time to check-in, yet you discover that the flight has been overbooked. A call is made for volunteers to surrender their seats on the flight and travel on a later service. Only two passengers go forward. You are then selected by the crew to wait for the next flight. Under EU law you are entitled to compensation but you were returning home for a special event and no monetary reward can improve your mood.

This is the letter lots of people would send:

Dear Mr [chief executive],

I am absolutely furious at Acme Air and I want to vent my spleen. Last week, I was due to fly from Birmingham to Amsterdam on the 14.10hrs service, in order to attend the surprise birthday celebrations of my aunt who lives just outside of the city. The event was due to start at 18.00hrs CET, and having booked many weeks ago, I had more than enough time to get there.

However, when I turned up to check-in, I was greeted by a completely moronic member of your staff who rudely told me that the flight had been overbooked and therefore I could not fly! If I could have punched her there and then I would. She could not put me on another flight until 22.00hrs, which meant that I would miss the party. Having given her a piece of my mind, she said I was entitled to compensation, quoting a figure of roughly £50.

Is this how your stupid company treats its loyal customers?? You can be sure I will never fly with your airline EVER again. As for your £50 you can stick it where the sun does not shine.

I want you to properly compensate me, because the way you and your staff treat people is disgusting.

Yours sincerely

Scott Colvin

It would be much better to send something like this:

Dear Mr [chief executive],

I am writing to you as a last resort, having endured an especially poor customer experience with your airline last week. I have used the suggested channels of contact with your customer services department, but I find my complaint has not progressed so I would like to see if you will assist me instead.

I was due to fly from Birmingham to Amsterdam on the 14.10hrs service, in order to attend the surprise birthday celebrations of my aunt who lives just outside of the city.

The event was due to start at 18.00hrs CET, and having booked many weeks ago, I had more than enough time to get there.

However, when I turned up to check-in, I was told by a member of your staff that the flight had been overbooked and therefore I could not fly. She could not put me on another flight until 22.00hrs, which meant that I would miss the party.

I do understand that most airlines often sell more seats on an aircraft than are actually available. However, I do not believe sufficient effort was made to offer me an alternative given the importance of my visit to Amsterdam. The compensation was a secondary consideration, but the £50 on offer is clearly an inappropriate figure given the disruption your company's error caused.

I am seeking two things from you: firstly an apology for preventing me from taking my flight, and the distress caused by not being able to attend my family event. Secondly, I would like to receive the full compensation you are able to pay, namely €250 as per European legislation.

I am sure we can resolve this situation as soon as possible. Please note that I have copied the following people into this letter, as I am aware that you are currently undergoing a regulatory review and will be keen to demonstrate the responsiveness of your customer service: Rt Hon Theresa Villiers MP, the minister for aviation; Ed Davey, the minister for consumer affairs; Andrew Haines, the chief executive of the civil aviation authority; and my local MP, Sam Gyimah.

Yours sincerely

Scott Colvin

The key aim is to put the chief executive into a position where resistance is futile. The first letter would simply allow him to wriggle free because a) it is too personal and angry b) it is not clear what I am asking the chief executive to do and c) the letter is just sent to him which gives him the opportunity to ignore it. It comes across as unreasonable and is likely to convince a company to dig its heels in. The second letter adopts a firm but fair approach, with an implicit threat (i.e. the recognition that the airline is in the process of arguing for lower airport charges with the regulator). Navigating a path away from anger is always the best approach, expressing disappointment that it has required you to email a chief executive with a relatively minor request, yet emphasising that you want this to be resolved to your satisfaction.

Presenting your case clearly is especially important when you are dealing with politicians and major corporations, who invest a great deal of time and money developing and harnessing their communication skills. This is not always because it is their primary concern, but because the modern corporate and political world requires them to be able to demonstrate good presentational skills. A chief executive or a minister will, as a matter of course, receive professional media training at least once a year, and special training for major crises that might befall them. They will also often receive help in preparing for public press conferences or parliamentary committee hearings – every answer tested and agreed – plus sound bites and ways to avoid difficult questions. There are top communications agencies and in-house specialists who offer this service and can make a lot of money doing it, so it does mean when you target a politician or corporate leader you will usually be up against a savvy operator. This does not mean, in the course of your complaints and campaigns, that you should not speak with your own voice (in fact, as I shall demonstrate, this can work to your advantage). But it does mean that poor communication can damage your chances of getting what you want, when you want it.

The power of blogging

One way of publicly logging your grievances (or at least using the threat of it as a means to persuade) is to make use of the opportunity to create a blog site to detail your poor customer experience. The term 'blog' is a blend of its formal name 'web log' and is best described as an internet page which is managed by an individual who provides commentary on issues, either of a personal nature or on a particular topic such as politics, fashion, or celebrity gossip. The information tends to be updated frequently, with many blogs refreshed several times a day. A blog which goes quiet for too long will simply disappear from view. The thought of reading the ill-informed views of a guy in his bedroom probably fills you with horror, but such sites do not tend to come to prominence. In politics and business, the best blogs get literally hundreds of thousands of 'hits' each week. The best examples they include the BBC's Robert Peston and Nick Robinson, as well as Guido Fawkes and the *Financial Times*. In the case of Peston, he has explained that he blogs in order to provide more depth to the big business stories of the day, given that television and radio usually require short and snappy headlines. The best blogs match the quality of analysis and insight which can be found in the quality daily newspapers; the worst peddle rumour and half-truths as clear fact.

They are useful to a campaign because anybody with access to a computer and an internet connection can create and compile one in less than thirty minutes. The potential of the internet to challenge established companies is staggering, and will only become more and more influential. What astonishes me further is how ill-equipped so many companies are in relation to social media. Many big firms in the FTSE-100 will still ban their staff from using Facebook or Twitter in the office, but they are missing the point. Turning your back on sites which are shaping and changing the way we communicate to each other in the hope that they will go away is naïve at best and dangerous at worst. The genie is out of the bottle and companies will benefit from their staff better understanding the possibilities of the sites. If a customer threatens someone that they will post their complaints on Twitter, it would help if the staff member knew what it was and therefore what damage can be inflicted.

They can be a tremendously useful way of keeping a community campaign bubbling along too, and it can encourage your supporters to stay in touch and keep up to date with developments.

Why do complaints fail?

Complaining is something most of us are really bad at. We all do it on a daily basis but almost always ineffectively. Bad customer service gets us angry as consumers and we respond by shouting at a representative of the company and making idle threats or we lose our bottle and whinge to others instead without confronting the real problem.

The key reasons why we fail:

› We use verbal aggression (for example, getting personal or using bad language).
› We use physical aggression (threaten to punch or hit someone).
› Our arguments are not watertight (we do not anticipate the counter arguments we are going to face and then flounder).
› We aim too high (we go straight to the chief executive, but fire off a poorly written letter without copying anyone in to it).
› We aim too low (we make do with the call operative on the minimum wage, and expect them to be able to change company policy.)
› We give up too early (we suddenly decide that the stress of complaining is 'not worth it').

The initial thing you need to keep in mind is that call centre operatives and even customer services managers are trained to be resistant. The days of the customer is always right are long gone, so be prepared to hunker down and get stuck in. The ultra-important point remains: be polite. That doesn't mean friendly. It just means that you do not descend to insulting or belittling the other person on the phone. But also work out what it is that the company is likely to say to you when you argue your case. For instance, they might say that there is no record of the conversation you claim took place, that the rules clearly stated the outcome you have complained about, finishing with a 'What do you want us to do about it?'

A company has a huge advantage over you as a consumer. In their attempts to remove risk, they will have thought about every likely scenario and prepared an excuse. But just keep in mind that ultimately it is not cost effective for them to continue to resist a small claim if you show no sign of backing off. You just need to be asking the right person. A customer services apparatchik with no freedom to take decisions is obviously not going to be able to satisfy your complaint, which is why you need to punch higher.

What really stresses consumers is that every attempt to contact a call centre makes you feel powerless and not in control. The call is at the mercy of an operative who can't really help (other than to read information from a screen), and could cut you off or put you on hold for several minutes at a time. How many times have you been forced to go through all of your personal data just to pass a security check and then be told that you have come through to the wrong department, and will have to be transferred? You have to then provide all the same information for a second time. There is no point complaining because more often than not the members of the call centre are just hired hands who do not even directly work for the company in question.

Not having data to hand is a basic error which the call

operative can then exploit as you become flustered and scramble around for bits of paper. Simply write out a list of the key facts in advance of any call, such as:

1. A reference number or date of last correspondence.
2. The name of the person or department you need to speak to.
3. A brief history of the case so far, in short bullet points.
4. The details (if you need them) of the politicians and third parties who you will contact if you do not get satisfaction in your complaint.
5. A clear line of what you would like to happen next.

It might look like:

1. Scott Colvin – ref: 2567/789
2. Angela Bates, Customer Services Director
3. Due to fly Birmingham to Amsterdam on the 14.10hrs service on flight RYR210; discovered at check-in desk that flight was full and not offered alternative flight until 22.00hrs the following morning; spoken to rudely by airline staff so asked to speak to customer services representative, but was told nobody was available to see me
4. Key targets include transport secretary Philip Hammond, consumer affairs minister Ed Davey and local MP Sam Gyimah
5. I expect an apology for the experience, and compensation for costs incurred by forced overnight stay at the airport

The reason why this type of interaction is more stressful than even a confrontation in a shop is the feeling of utter powerlessness. Speaking to a customer services operative is the only way of contacting the company yet you know that whoever you speak with is going to frustrate you. Every time the company gets you to give up, it saves them money (at least in the short term).

The minister for consumer affairs

Let me introduce you to one of the most helpful people in your quest for justice from the corporate world, namely the minister for consumer affairs. The position falls within the Department for Business, Innovation and Skills, which sets policy for the business sector and also has responsibility for employment relations and postal affairs. Have you ever heard of the name Ed Davey? Gareth Thomas? Melanie Johnson? Kevin Brennan? Trust me, you do not need to feel embarrassed if you have not, but they are all former holders of this post. Given that consumer issues are so important to people up and down the country, you might be surprised to learn that very few people approach them in this role, aside from the odd speaking engagement. It is a position in government which tends to be given to a middle-ranking minister, many of whom never quite make it into the Cabinet.

Even people who work in politics would often struggle to name the minister who is responsible for consumers, yet I have used the holders of this office to my advantage when battling with companies, and so can you. Their lack of profile actually works in your favour, because the corporate world is especially fearful of the unknown. If you are in a dispute with your credit card company and you threaten to report them to David Cameron or George Osborne, it is unlikely that they will believe you. Everyone knows that Prime Ministers or Chancellor of the Exchequers are too busy running the country to spend time solving your specific consumer or community issues. But it sounds all too plausible that the minister for consumer affairs might be persuaded to stick their two-penneth in.

The various holders of this office will no doubt have been puzzled at the number of times they have been copied into emails and letters I have sent to corporations, but they are a classic example of how to use politicians passively. There is not a single occasion when the minister has responded to a message I have sent or chased up a company as I have requested, but I did not expect them to. To be annoyed by the lack of a response is missing the point because just having their name attached to an email or letter of complaint is enough to give you the leverage to succeed.

To find the name of the current minister check the website of the Department of Business, Innovation and Skills (www. bis.gov.uk). On the homepage there is a tab marked 'Ministers' where you'll find a list of the full ministerial team. It will also list the policy responsibilities for each of the top team, so you will be able to see who the current consumer affairs minister is. As I will demonstrate, name-dropping this minister on the telephone or into an email can literally change the game in your future battles.

On a brief tangent, it is a missed opportunity that the holders of this role are not more prominent in our day-to-day lives. As a society we have become interested in consumer-focused media, such as the BBC's *Watchdog*, Channel 4's *Undercover Boss* or *Mary Portas: Secret Shopper*. But why should it be television personalities who step into the breach to stick up for us? The consumer affairs minister should be all over the airwaves, speaking up for everyday people, actively taking on bad examples of customer service. Taking a more populist stance in this area would go some way to help justify why such roles exist to the general public.

The pressure point

A pressure point in the field of martial arts refers to an area on the human body which may produce significant pain or other effects when manipulated in a specific manner. Before you head upstairs to dust off your nunchucks, I am not about to suggest physically beating a chief executive or politician is a good way to proceed. But as with an opponent in battle, each chief executive, chairman, shop worker, MP or councillor has a pressure point. These pressure points can be manipulated to render your opponent powerless to resist your campaign. Well, most of the time. Let me give you some examples:

a) If you are a chief executive of a water company, one of your pressure points is your relationship with Ofwat, the regulator, and their pricing reviews which cover a five-year period. Without a good regulatory outcome (the ability to charge consumers more than they had previously), the CEO's future at the company and subsequent reputation will be damaged. The share price will fall and their competitors could gain an advantage. So one of the key pressure points in this instance is anything which might embarrass him/her in the eyes of the regulatory body.

b) If you run a more dynamic, unregulated company then the pressure point is the general reputation amongst customers. Anything that could influence the perception of the company, and thereby impact the bottom line through a loss of customers matters a great deal to these types of firms.

c) If you are an MP, you are constantly fighting for your career in a whole range of ways – with your local association, with your constituents, with your opposition candidates, with your party whips and with your parliamentary colleagues. So the pressure points are multiple and can be used in a variety of ways. A bad speech, a newspaper exposé, a fall out with activists, negative letters in the local paper, community petitions etc., will make an MP sit up and take notice.

d) Even for backbench MPs (i.e. those who have no ministerial or shadow ministerial responsibilities), who might be perceived as having less to lose, bad publicity could lead to the loss of their seat either at the next election, or simply by falling out with the local association. Two examples of this: in 1997 Neil Hamilton did not just lose his parliamentary seat in the leafy idyll of Tatton, he was thrashed. The local party stuck by him throughout the 'Cash for Questions' scandal and subsequent court case, but the voters felt that he had behaved appallingly and duly tossed him out; in April 2004 the Conservative MP for Surrey Heath (one of the safest seats in the country) Nick Hawkins was de-selected by his own local party members. Not because of an expenses scandal, but simply because he was not seen to be capable of achieving high office in the future. It is significant that his replacement, Michael Gove, is now in one of the top offices of government.

e) The moment you become a frontbench MP, either in government or in opposition, you immediately become a target. Everything you have ever said publicly will be scanned and scrutinised, and you are always just one wrong move away from waving goodbye to your political career. Former home secretary Jacqui Smith was perceived to be a talented and capable minister in the summer of 2007, perhaps even with the potential to be Prime Minister one day. Within two years she was voted out at the 2010 general election, her reputation tarnished forever. That was because it came to light that she had not only entered a range of expenses claims for items such as a flat screen TV and scatter cushions, but had also designated her constituency home as not being her main residence (despite her own claims to the contrary on her website). Although she was hardly the only MP to make dubious residency claims, her real downfall was the small matter of two pornographic pay-per-view movies which were charged to the taxpayer. The fact it was her husband who proved to be responsible did not make the story any less embarrassing. The pressure point for a frontbencher is therefore any issue which has the potential to stain a minister's CV.

f) Finding an MEP's pressure point is more difficult as they tend to be less connected with the day-to-day goings on in their region. But the lack of attention they receive in comparison to their Westminster counterparts makes them more likely to throw themselves in to any opportunity for publicity. This is almost a reverse pressure point, namely that the insatiable desire to be noticed by anybody is helpful when enlisting their support.

g) If you are a councillor, you probably feel less pressure in regards to your political career. Being a councillor can be the start of a path which leads to Parliament, but the pressures are moderate unless you sit on one of the big metropolitan councils such as Liverpool, Birmingham or Manchester. But councillors are no different to their Westminster counterparts when it comes to election time. They do not want to lose so the pressure point is anything which might trigger negative media coverage in the local and regional press and cost them the chance of being re-elected.

Harnessing these pressure points for your own advantage as a consumer is easy, as long as you take the time to consider how to adapt to the situation in which you find yourself. To bring these techniques to life, let us look at some examples of consumer battles I have encountered, how I went about solving them and the lessons you too can learn. Please note that I have not revealed the names of the companies because it is the principles of campaigning we are considering, rather than obsessing about each particular corporate brand.

Case study: The gas boiler

If there is one single example of a consumer situation which I have been in, and solved, then it is the example of my dealings with an energy company a few years ago. We had bought a new build house, partly because of the advantages of having a property with brand new fixtures and fittings. One of those features was a gas-fired central heating system. Despite only being two years old, the boiler packed up. It was frustrating to say the least especially as it was still winter. Fortunately I had taken out boiler insurance cover with a major provider, so did not foresee any significant problems. The company agreed to send someone out the following morning, especially important as my children were still very young and we had an obvious need for hot water and heating.

However, the engineer was left looking rather puzzled by

the problem and said he could not fix it on the spot. He would instead call the following day. The next day, he did indeed call, but with bad news. He explained that the part he needed for our boiler was not in stock and also difficult to source, as it was made in a particular factory in France. He assured me he would put in an order immediately for the part, and asked me to call the customer service line in the coming days to check progress. I was disappointed but the prognosis was not unreasonable.

So I called, twice a day but with no clearer idea of when the problem would be solved, the frustration building with every repetition of the holding music and encounter with surly folks manning the call centre. This went on for several days and eventually I had to move my family out of the house to my in-laws who kindly took pity on us.

The frustration of having a busy job, knowing that my children couldn't live in their own home whilst this saga continued became too much to take. There was one day in particular which signalled the low point in this whole sorry episode. I was sat in a coffee shop with my mobile clamped to my ear, the sweat building as I was on the telephone for nearly an hour, being passed from clueless person to person, department to department. I was told that I just had to be patient and would be contacted when the part becomes available. I demanded to speak to someone senior, and was told no one was available. Eventually I persuaded them to put me through to someone who could record my complaint. The phone went silent, and then cut off completely. With my temple throbbing and my face flushed with anger, I had to dial again and restart the entire process.

Having spoken to someone who claimed to be senior, I logged my complaint but was told that it could be a further two weeks before the part would become available. The lady told me 'we cannot do anything more for you until then, sir' and then the phone went down. As the day progressed, and having broken the news to my family that we were unlikely to be able to return home for another couple of weeks, my anger evolved into steely determination. Stomping around the lounge muttering dark words under my breath, it suddenly came to me, like a vision. What would I advise a client to do if they came to me with this scenario? I grabbed a sheet of paper and began to sketch out a plan designed to answer the fundamental question, namely how to get the company to fix my problem within the current two week waiting time.

I knew the name of the chief executive of the company and managed to track down his email address. But I was realistic. An email to the CEO of one of the UK's biggest companies about a boiler part issue was unlikely to get much of a response, and would probably get handed down to a customer complaints assistant, exactly the same type of person I had struggled with for several days already. So I decided to copy a few others into my email. Knowing that the company in question was regulated, I realised that the two people the CEO really did not wish to involve in my incident were the chief executive of the energy regulator, the Office of the Gas and Electricity Markets (OFGEM), and the chief executive of the sector watchdog Energywatch (now part of a new entity called Consumer Focus). So I copied them both in to the email. But this still did not feel heavy enough and I knew I only had one shot at this. So I included my local Member of Parliament who was at that time a member of the shadow Cabinet, and the minister for consumer affairs at the Department of Business, Innovation and Skills (BIS). I then wrote a balanced, non-ranting email, sent more in sorrow than in anger.

You will note that I included a further threat which will have given the CEO further food for thought, namely that I would start a blog site in which I would document my day-to-day customer experiences with the company. This is the type of site which can really get attention from other bloggers but also from the media.

Calmly explaining why I felt forced into doing this, I simply asked for the CEO's direct help in cutting through the bureaucracy. I have blanked out the company's name but the email read:

Dear Mr ——,

An email directed to the chief executive of —— may seem like a hammer to crack a nut.

However, I write to you in utter desperation after ten days of poor service from —— and I have therefore taken the 'nuclear' option. This is predominantly because I have a three month old baby and a 2.5 year old, and we have no heating or hot water.

My boiler broke down on Saturday, 17 March. I called —— and an engineer arrived the next day.

He told me the problem was a broken pump, and easily fixed. The boiler would therefore be fixed the following Tuesday.

That day came and went and the engineer did not come. When he arrived the next day (Wednesday) he told my wife that actually it was a bigger problem getting the part and therefore may be a couple more days.

That time came and went, and I called again to be told that the part was on special order. It would take a few more days. The Parts team were requested to call me to give a definitive date – they didn't bother to call. The weekend has passed and no progress.

I called yet again today, and was promised that the Parts people would confirm a date when the part would be ready. Once again, they did not bother to call.

Suddenly, I am now told that the part is out of stock and could therefore take a long time to arrive. I was told not to keep calling but just to wait.

I don't think it is acceptable for my very young children to cope without heat or hot water for such a very long time. The lack of clarity, of responsiveness, from —— just compounds the problem. I intend to set up a blog site recording my problems with —— on a day-to-day basis, and perhaps it will attract some attention.

In the meantime I have copied this email to my MP, Peter Ainsworth, the consumer affairs minister Gareth Thomas MP, the chief executive of Energywatch and the chief executive of OFGEM.

I would appreciate your intervention in this matter.

Kind regards, Scott Colvin

With one click of the mouse, it was sent, and although I suspected that I would hear nothing again, my MP responded quickly the following morning, copied to all, expressing his concern at my situation and asking for a clear update to how my complaint would be dealt with. After a day of silence, an email pinged into my inbox, from the chief executive himself. He apologised profusely for what had happened. But here's the really good bit. He revealed that he had ordered his team to manufacture the missing boiler part overnight at a factory in France. The part was to be sent to my house by courier in the early hours of the morning, at which point the company's two most senior engineers would come and install the part, not leaving until they were certain the problem was fixed.

Just to be absolutely sure, my case was being passed to the most senior customer services director who would be calling me before and after the repair was made, to ensure I was happy with the experience. Finally, an additional engineer would come and ensure that all systems were working and check the rest of the heating system free of charge. Just thirty-six hours after my email, the heating was pumping and the water was hot. The family were moved back in and victory was mine. I have an important point to make, incidentally. Once everything was working again, I took the time to email the CEO directly, copied in to the others, and thanked him for his personal intervention. You could take the attitude that he only acted out of self-interest, but I believe strongly that if someone does the right thing, you need to acknowledge it. Otherwise, the person who has made the extra effort has less incentive to do so again in the future. One of the big mistakes made by pressure groups of all sorts is the mean way they mark success in their campaigns. Rather than thank those involved for making the right decision or changing their minds on an issue, many groups use it as a further opportunity to either punish the decision-makers or then go on to push for something else.

You could again take the view I got lucky, that it was a one-off, and I had found the right CEO at the right time. But you are wrong. The principles behind the boiler story perfectly encapsulate the reasons why you too should adopt lobbying skills to empower yourself, and how you can use these principles in a whole host of consumer situations. Let us deconstruct why the above worked:

> I went **direct to the CEO**. He is the ultimate decision-maker for the business and will get few direct emails from customers. I sent my email late at night, which meant he was more likely to pick it up when he left for the office at 6.30am. If you send your email during late morning or early afternoon, it is much more likely to be intercepted by the PA or secretary.

> The email was **copied into people** he would have referred to as 'key stakeholders', namely his regulator, sector watchdog, consumer affairs minister and a member of the shadow Cabinet. This made it much less likely that my complaint could be ignored.

> I also kept my email **constructive and reasonable**, because otherwise you lose the argument before it has begun and force stubborn leaders to drag their heels.

> I included a **further threat** which it was realistic for me to follow-up on, namely starting a blog site to document the poor customer experience I had received.

› In response to the CEO's intervention I followed up the email with a thank you. This is always the right thing to do, as it rewards good behaviour and makes it more likely the company will behave similarly in the future.

Case study: The Gatwick Express

Bringing together and organising advocates for your cause is extremely important. I used to work for the company that formally owned the Gatwick Express train service. As you may know, the train runs directly from the airport to London Victoria and is an invaluable lifeline to tourists looking to get into central London quickly, rather than using the standard train service which runs concurrently but takes an extra twenty minutes or so. It has won several awards, most notably as Best Train Company in the country, since it was privatised in 1994. But it became clear that a number of rail officials at the Department for Transport felt under pressure to deliver more commuter services on the Brighton Mainline. It can cause great stress and confusion for people to not only be packed like sardines on a rush hour train, but to also see half empty airport express trains racing their way into London. Generally speaking it is the role of governments to develop transport policies which benefit the majority in most instances, but there were other internal politics at play, namely a battle between those responsible for rail and those for aviation within the department.

This whole saga meant that Gatwick Express would effectively cease to exist. The train would no longer be a non-stop service which would mean considerably longer journey times, no special place for luggage, and a toxic mix of stressed rush hour commuters and suitcase-laden tourists competing for seats. The analysis showed that it would force more cars onto the road, as tourists would head into London by car instead of suffering a stressful train ride.

This dilemma had been vexing a variety of government ministers, but eventually fell to one man to decide, the then

Secretary of State for Transport, Douglas Alexander MP. Alexander was riding high at the time as a personal favourite of Gordon Brown, who was just months away from finally replacing his nemesis Tony Blair; by any analysis, Alexander had a bright future ahead.

Within the aviation industry, lots of people thought the writing was on the wall for the Gatwick Express, with only moderate effort being employed to fight for its future. They were effectively going through the motions, even though a new transport minister meant a new opportunity. I took the view that if we could identify his pressure point, we could exploit it. What would go through Alexander's mind when he opened the ministerial red box and read his officials' advice? What could we do to make him nervous about signing the piece of paper which would wipe the train service from existence?

The key lay in the point I made earlier about Alexander being one of Brown's most trusted advisers. With Blair now weeks away from departing Downing Street, Brown wanted to avoid a challenge in his attempt to finally become Labour leader. From Alexander's perspective, a Brown government would mean a plum job and a place in the inner circle. The only thing that could prevent that from happening was a screw up, or falling out of favour with Labour backbenchers. So Alexander presumably became increasingly risk-averse, with the aim of keeping his department ticking along and avoiding any controversy.

With that in mind, we started to target Labour backbenchers to support the campaign and then exert pressure upon the minister, but we first had to identify which MPs cared enough about the issue to act. Working with a Conservative MP to sponsor it, we used an Early Day Motion to find a number of Labour MPs willing to publicly support it. Once tabled, other MPs started signing it too, from the Conservatives to the Liberal Democrats and a surprising number of representatives from Northern Ireland (explained by the number of MPs who flew into Gatwick, rather than Heathrow). This significant body of cross-party support gave us a base to work with, and we contacted each MP, especially the Labour members, to urge them to write directly to the minister.

This decision was also taking place in the warm afterglow of London winning the right to host the 2012 Olympics and I spotted a tiny footnote in the submission document produced by the UK government to win the bid. It boasted that the centre of London could be reached from Gatwick in just half an hour, so scrapping the service would mean a broken promise. Admittedly, this would not have represented a Watergate-level political blunder, but the question was whether Douglas Alexander wanted to be the person responsible for breaking one of the bid's pledges. Building on this, and to create further publicity, Virgin Atlantic boss Richard Branson agreed to write an opinion piece in the influential London newspaper, the *Evening Standard*, and his high profile heaped additional pressure of the watching Alexander.

The result was a good one. With a minor concession of the trains running south of Gatwick to Brighton at certain points of the day, the service was saved with Alexander commenting that 'this is good news for both rail and air passengers'.

So what can be applied from this case study to your campaigns?

›   Think very carefully about the **decision-maker** you are trying to influence. What have they got to lose by making the wrong choice? How can you exploit that fear?

›   What are the **benefits** of your preferred outcome? Work out the top three or so arguments as to why your view should prevail.

›   Work hard to **identify all of your supporters** as early as possible. As with the MPs from Northern Ireland, your potential supporters might not seem obvious at first.

› Try and **find a broken promise** that your opponent is about to make/has made. The British sense of fair play means that we like people to keep their word, and if you can find evidence that someone has said one thing and done another, then it could just give you an edge.

› As with Richard Branson supporting the Gatwick train, always try to get a **senior voice** to support your campaign, wherever possible. It might be a politician, a local business leader, or a community figure such as a vicar. A prominent supporter buys you extra kudos in the eyes of the decision-maker.

Case study: The pizza

When my wife Hannah was heavily pregnant with our first child (in fact, she was just weeks away from giving birth), we ordered a takeaway pizza from a well-known outlet. Half-way through eating our pizza, Hannah found an unwanted ingredient: a large lump of glass. Luckily she managed to spit it out before it cut her mouth, or even worse, had swallowed it.

I called the store immediately and told the shop assistant what had happened. In his panic, the guy admitted that a bulb in one of the shop's ovens had exploded that evening. Yet he and his colleagues had presumed that none had infiltrated the boxed pizzas, so the product still got dispatched without having been properly checked. Outraged, I contacted the HQ of the pizza chain. Unbelievably, the response I received by post entirely contradicted what the shop assistant responsible had told me. But that was far from the most shocking content in the letter. In order to persuade me to end my complaint, the company offered me £25 worth of free pizza from the same company. Having picked my jaw off of the floor, I decided that I had a responsibility to ensure the safety of other customers. This was not about compensation; it was about teaching the company a lesson.

At the time I was a local councillor, which was helpful but not the sole reason why I was able to exact my revenge. As a first step, I called the environmental health officer at the town hall and recounted the story, asking for them to investigate the incident. This is not something they only do for councillors, so if you ever find yourself in this situation you should always report the food outlet. The official was very helpful and he paid a surprise visit to the store to fully investigate how the restaurant managed its food preparation. The pleasure of imagining the faces of the staff as the clipboard-wielding man from the council walked through the doors was immense.

As a second step, I also reported what had happened to the elected councillor, or 'portfolio holder' who was responsible for environmental health. This meant that any correspondence to the pizza chain would include a senior councillor's name attached, which would especially concern the management at head office.

The council officer reported back and the findings were very interesting. The shop workers had admitted that the bulb had exploded during the peak evening period, but that no one bothered to check the pizzas which had been boxed but were still sat inside the oven to keep warm. In fact, the lump of glass had fired directly through the hole in the side of the pizza box. Even worse, the council officer had discovered that the requisite training had not been given to staff on what to do in such incidents, which was further negligence on the part of the management. The officer then said he would write to the managing director of the company outlining his concerns, which he did and copied me into.

At this stage, I knew that the facts of the incident had been confirmed, and actual safety improvements to be put in place (to protect other local customers from a similar fate), which was the key aim. However, the response to the council officer came back and was full of factual inaccuracies. Despite the staff members admitting full liability for the broken glass, the management took a different position claiming that all pizzas had been fully checked before being sent out for delivery.

The council officer was annoyed by this and ensured that the company was given a good dressing down for its behaviour, forcing it to implement a costly training programme for the store with immediate effect.

But the company's management still needed to be taught a lesson. I knew what would hurt them the most: negative publicity. I called the big regional paper to tell them what had happened, and put a particular emphasis on the fact my wife had been pregnant at the time (our little boy had now been safely delivered). Unsurprisingly, the journalist loved the story and wanted us to head down to the paper's offices immediately. However, this story clearly worked best not as a local politician who was angry, but as a concerned pregnant woman whose unborn child had been at threat by the negligence of a well-recognised national food brand.

She has not yet fully forgiven me, but my wife begrudgingly agreed to have a sizeable photograph of her and our son appear in the paper, with a large headline which read 'When I knew I had bitten into glass, I went a bit hysterical'. The story took up most of a broadsheet-sized page. The impact of that story, in the area in which the store operated, unquestionably put some people off ordering from that chain, so I knew I had caused them a direct financial hit. With the publicity over, I sent a letter to the company's managing director complete with a photocopy of the newspaper story. This was one occasion when it was okay to take pleasure in teaching a company director a lesson, so I reminded him of the implications of treating customers with such disdain.

So can we take anything from this case study to apply to instances where you are not trying to get compensation or a refund, but simply seeking an apology and/or getting your revenge?

› It is important to try to **begin your complaint in the formal way,** via a letter to the company to seek a fulsome apology. Sometimes, companies do the right thing and you should give them a chance to demonstrate that. If I had been the managing director in this instance, I would have written to the complainant with a full, unreserved apology; made it clear what changes would be made in the store, especially training, to ensure it does not happen again; and I would have probably offered them some financial compensation too, even if it was agreed to give it to charity instead.

› Do not get bogged down in an exchange of letters with the company if you can find an **official outlet of complaint.** In this instance, the council official was only too happy to investigate, and he had powers to enforce fines and penalties upon the company if he deemed them to be negligent.

› Once the concerns you have about a company's performance have begun to be addressed to protect others, you should **harness the local media** to deliver a knockout blow. There is no harm in talking to a journalist first to assess how interesting or not the story might be. They will give you an honest assessment as to whether it would be followed up.

› **Get the last word** by letting them know how you have responded to the original incident for which they were to blame. Write to the chief executive or managing director and coolly explain why their customer service fell short and what they need to do to fix it. It is, at the very least, a nice feeling to hit back.

Case study: The clamper

If you were to think of the most challenging consumer situation you could find yourself in, negotiating with a burly man attaching a wheel clamp to your front tyre would presumably feature high on your list. But arguably my most miraculous example of the power of lobbying was one summer's day in my former hometown. At the time I was working for the local MP, who also happened to have the job title of shadow minister for local government; fear not, this does have a relevance to my story. Having parked up at the nearby train station to pick up some publicity photographs for my MP, I returned to find a clamper applying the apparatus of his trade to my wheel. With a heavy heart, I asked him what he was doing, which I admit seems a silly question in retrospect. Initially he was very aggressive, as presumably his job entails receiving a great deal of personal abuse, even though most of us would consider it to be justified. But I stayed calm, and gently asked him how I was supposed to know that I would be clamped if I parked in this spot. He pointed out a sign which was about five inches high and positioned twenty yards away informing me that clampers were in operation.

Anyone who has ever been busted by a clamping firm will no doubt criticise the way in which they operate. The henchmen sit in unmarked vans and will happily watch an elderly lady innocently parking only to swoop in once the poor victim has walked away. Within a few minutes a clamp is fitted, with costs totalling hundreds of pounds if you include the vehicle being towed away to a depot. There is little you can do at this stage other than pay up, utterly furious and without grounds for complaint.

I asked him how much money was required to get the car released. He told me it would be £80. I then proceeded to walk away and he seemed surprised. 'Where are you going?' he said. 'To get you your money,' I replied. But, in a scene reminiscent of an episode of the hit TV detective series *Columbo*, I turned to ask him one final question. I requested the name of his boss. 'Why do you ask?' he said, to which I calmly replied that I worked for a senior politician with an interest in local government issues, especially the wheel-clamping industry.

The reason I need your boss's name, I said, was so I could ensure it is spelled and pronounced correctly when my MP reads it out in a forthcoming parliamentary debate on your industry. But, I quickly added, I understand that you are just doing your job and I am sure that your boss will not hold you personally responsible. Frowning, he eyed me suspiciously, and then knelt down and proceeded to remove the clamp. Having done so, he said: 'I would not normally be able to do this but as you were very polite, I'll make an exception.'

Ok, so a number of things are running through your mind. Firstly, I did genuinely work for an MP at the time, and you almost certainly do not. That obviously provided an opportunity for me to put pressure on him, especially as it was true that my boss was indeed interested in the activities of wheel-clampers. Secondly, if this situation were replicated another nine times, the clamp would probably have remained on the car. No doubt I got lucky.

However, there are lessons to be learned:

› When you are faced with an injustice from a company, you must **stay calm**, even though the natural response is to get nasty in return. Firstly, it gives you the moral high ground in your dispute which always comes in handy as your complaint progresses up the chain; secondly, as with the car clamper, there is a small chance that remaining calm and polite could work to your advantage and help to solve the problem at that moment. The same could apply to parking wardens. The response they expect to writing out a ticket fine is the threat of physical or verbal abuse. That type of response will never, ever make them change their decision to place the ticket onto your windscreen. However, staying calm and being polite might just tip the balance in your favour. It does happen from time to time, as I have demonstrated.

› Try to **think on your feet** in any given situation. This is not always easy but by giving the impression that you know something about consumer law or the political process, for example, will make the person you are dealing with a little uneasy. By name-dropping the name of an MP, and suggesting that he had views on the wheel-clamping industry, was enough to make the man believe that fixing the apparatus carried a risk. You can use similar techniques when you are speaking to a company by phone or writing by letter.

› If you have more time than I did, try to do some **research** into your consumer rights, by contacting the consumer bodies I mentioned earlier.

Case study: The wine company

A few years ago, I received one of those offers which always seem to be too good to be true, namely to join an online wine club with lots of free booze with your first order. Having casually read the contract details it seemed that the promise was of no obligations or hassles.

I fell for it, hook, line and sinker. Having received my case of wine and happily sampling its delights, I did not notice the smallest of small prints which stated that unless I specifically notified the company, they would continue to send me a case of wine each month at a higher price than I could buy it in my local off-licence. This is exactly what they did a few weeks later, and I was lumbered with a box of unwanted wine with £120 to pay. So I called the amusingly titled 'customer helpline' and explained that I had not asked for this wine, and that the rules had not been made clear to me when I joined. 'Hard cheese, sir' was effectively the response I got back. The young lady I spoke to had clearly fielded several hundred of these calls in her short career, given the weary tone in her voice.

Having battled with this particular person for thirty

minutes, it was time to roll out the technique that I have been outlining so far in this book. She was clearly not the decision-maker, so there was not much point in flogging the proverbial dead horse with her. I asked to speak to the most senior person in the call centre. I was told that the office manager was busy and therefore unavailable to come to the telephone.

I never believe this particular excuse to be true but decided to play along with it. So I asked if I could leave a message, and could she write it down as it was very important. It simply read 'Your company's approach to customer service is unethical and I shall be raising it with the minister for consumer affairs when I see him next week. Please call me before that conversation takes place if you would like to clarify your company's policy.' Before you pick me up for lying, I was not. I was being disingenuous which is not quite the same. By chance I was genuinely attending an event at which this minister would be present, at which he was giving a speech, albeit with another thirty or so people. The operative was seemingly distracted by what I had asked her to write down, and I could make out some muffled noises as she put her hand over the phone. Suddenly, she decided that it was okay after all; I could have a full refund, and it would be processed the very same day.

Why did this work?

> I insisted that someone **more senior** than the call centre operative became involved in my complaint. That is not good for the more junior person because presumably it does not reflect well on their own ability to handle unhappy customers.

> In the absence of a regulator or some other influential body, I **name-dropped** a junior minister who they would never have heard of but will have troubled the supervisor. The supervisor was also keen to ensure that this complaint did not gain momentum; after all what is £120 to a major

company of this size? Is the supervisor really going to call my bluff over such a relatively small amount of money? Ultimately, a company like that will get hundreds of such complaints each day, so yours has to stand out from the crowd.

> ›   I stayed **focused on the aspect of the complaint** which was unfair, namely that the explanation of the subscription system was badly written and potentially misleading.

Case study: The house builder

Once my eldest son had got a bit bigger, we needed to move and find more space to raise a family. We found a new development of just eleven houses in a nice, leafy part of Surrey.

Anyone who has ever bought a new build property will be familiar with the word 'snagging'. House builders, in order to maximise their profit margin, understandably try to work at full capacity. This means that they encourage their builders to get a development built as quickly as possible to cut the costs of manpower. That does not mean they do not take care over what they are doing (after all, if they continually made shoddy buildings, consumers would begin to notice and stop buying them), but it does mean that no house is 100 per cent perfect when you move in.

When the house is eventually sold, the occupants get a defined period of time to request improvements from the house builder, before being passed over to the National House Building Council (NHBC) for a ten year period of cover. The snagging might be a lick of paint, fixing a door handle, or something more serious such as a structural problem. When I agreed to buy, the one major aspect to the property that was missing was turf in the back garden. It was not a deal breaker, and we were persuaded that it was easy to sort out.

When we did move in, we realised that the gardening firm whom the work had been sub-contracted to had come up with a novel solution. They had simply chucked the turf onto mud (still scattered with building materials from the house build), and then had made a cursory attempt to trample it down. Needless to say, it looked awful, akin to walking on a rug under which a child had hidden lots of toys. The grass was surely going to die a slow, painful death. Repeated attempts to get the company to fix the problem had failed to illicit any meaningful response. It became increasingly stressful because the company was digging its heels in, and with our warranties soon to run out we would incur our own repair costs.

It is when you have exhausted all formal avenues to complain that the nuclear option comes into play. I tracked down the name and address of the company's regional director, and I outlined in moderate tones the difficulties I had faced, with a chronology of events and conversations which had previously taken place. I expressed great disappointment at the lack of customer service I had been given, but the key message to relay was that I was willing and able to take the complaint to the next level.

I did some research on the company with the aim of finding its pressure point. Imagine my joy when I discovered that they were seeking to complete the acquisition of a smaller rival. It was obvious that the last thing they would want was for this purchase to be derailed or made more costly by the negative media coverage I could garner. They wanted to keep the deal dull and uneventful. So I wrote to the regional director and outlined what I was going to do in the event that my requests were not granted.

Firstly, I would contact the local/regional media and create a story about the turf issue. Even if the paper was not willing to run a story, I could still get a letter published condemning the behaviour of the company and wondering aloud whether local people should therefore still welcome the potential merger.

Secondly, I would start a blog, outlining on a daily basis my experiences in trying to get the company to honour its promises. This would be easy to set up within a matter of minutes and would probably secure newspaper coverage in itself. This mimics a technique used by political parties and some companies, namely to leak details of an advert even if it does not actually exist. For example, if David Cameron were to announce a new tax rise, the opposition could tell a friendly journalist that they are preparing to launch a rebuttal ad. All it takes is for a designer to hastily draw something up and the journalist can then publish the ad and the story as an 'exclusive'. Of course, the political point has been made without the need to spend thousands of pounds putting the ad onto billboards or in newspapers. This happens all the time.

Lastly, I made it clear that I would also involve my local MP, the minister for consumer affairs, even the secretary of state for communities and local government and the shadow equivalent. Nobody on that list, except perhaps the local MP, would ever be likely to respond or get involved, but the house builder would not know that or at least not be willing to take the risk. Theirs is a sector which is especially scrutinised by government and have regulations imposed, at least before the coalition arrived.

The response was swift and satisfying. The work would be undertaken immediately, and we would be prioritised.

In summary, this approach worked because:

> I **identified the vulnerability** of the company at that point, namely the delicate negotiations to buy a small rival. Every company has a vulnerability of some description, but sometimes you can get lucky and the **right timing** helps your cause.

> I threatened to produce a snowstorm effect of bad publicity for the company, i.e. not just one negative hit, such as a single letter in the local newspaper, but a '**shock and awe**' strategy which would create real and tangible damage to the brand.

Conclusion

What I hope you have gathered from my case studies in this chapter is that there are a variety of techniques to getting what you want from the corporate world. Each and every one of the companies had failed to provide an acceptable level of service. They had all frustrated my efforts to get satisfaction in different ways, and they no doubt continue to do it to other people each and every day. When discussing the theme of this book with an MP before publication, they said that it is the system itself which needs to change rather than encouraging people to adopt 'vigilante' tactics. But how will this change present itself unless we begin to make it costly for companies to not do the right thing? Why should a consumer with children but without vital services such as heating and hot water sit and suffer in silence? I strongly believe that each and every one of us has got to start taking these organisations on at their own game. The countries which have a better tradition of complaining, such as the United States, also happen to have the biggest focus on customer service. In that country it is typical to tip people for a range of services, especially in a hotel or restaurant, but they do not reward poor behaviour, otherwise it would not create an incentive. In the UK, we almost always pay up regardless of the quality of the service we receive. Diners will sit and moan to one another about how poor an experience in a restaurant has been, but when asked if everything with the meal was OK, they tamely nod and pay the 12.5 per cent tip.

You should always ensure that you stand up for yourself, because on every occasion you decide to write off a company's error you are simply helping to perpetuate its cavalier attitude. They will not change unless we all collectively, yet individually, refuse to accept second best.

Chapter 5: Campaigning in your community

What is your campaign?

There are essentially three types of community campaigns you might find yourself involved in. Firstly, you might set out to pressurise a decision-maker by attempting to get a person or organisation to change their minds and prevent a decision from being taken. This might include reversing a decision to close an emergency unit at your local hospital or prevent a school playing field being sold off. This is the typical type of campaign and the one which tends to be the most interesting, although sometimes it can be perceived as negative; the term Not In My Back Yard (NIMBY) is North American in origin but is widely used in this country too as a derogatory term for any campaigners who oppose any proposed change in their area. These people will agree that new affordable housing needs to be built, just not near them; they might also take a hard line on law and order and want more prisons to be constructed, just not so close that it impacts the value of their own home.

Secondly, you might run a campaign to create grass roots support for a project not yet proposed, such as a new local library or children's play park. This type of initiative is obviously a great deal more positive. You are asking for something which would enhance your local community, and it is the type of campaign that is encouraged as part of

David Cameron's Big Society concept. The downside is that grass roots movements take a lot longer than grass does to grow. New projects usually mean a decision-maker having to find new money from already stretched budgets, so it can be a frustrating process for those engaged in community action.

Lastly, you might be trying to campaign to change behaviour or attitudes. This might include getting motorists to stop racing along your road. Lots of communities, for example, have even taken to purchasing their own mobile speed guns to try to make drivers think twice about breaking the speed limit. Once again, this type of programme can take longer, especially if the campaigners do not have the ability to directly fine motorists who break the law. However, national campaigns along this theme, such as making drivers wear their seatbelts or not drink and drive, have been phenomenally successful. In 1979, there were over 1,600 deaths caused by drink-driving; by 2009 it had fallen to below 400.

We should not categorise too clearly, as some campaigns may include elements of all three of the above. But you should begin your work in the community with a very clear sense of which type of campaign you are going to pursue. Too many people get an idea, run with it, but quickly lose direction and then interest. Unless you are already a party political type, you will not be looking for opportunities to campaign for the sakes of winning votes; you will be campaigning because the particular issue motivates you to do something about how you feel. Ultimately, if your child's local bus service to school was not threatened with being cut, you would probably not be campaigning to keep it open.

As your work progresses, it is inevitable that you will find yourself acting tactically to influence a decision, but in the early stages you should primarily focus on being strategic. Before deciding on a campaign, ask if it affects a lot of people. Is it just a few individuals on your road, or is it potentially going to affect everyone who lives in the town or county?

Does it affect a particular group of people, such as pensioners, women, an ethnic minority or single parents?

When you have answered that question, you also need to think what the real benefits would be for people who support your cause. If that is an easy thing to do, you should take the time to write down the clear goals and aims. If you have not got this part right, then the campaign is unlikely to progress. You should identify your campaign aims and work to a clear time frame. It is very helpful in gathering support if there are definite dates to push towards. For example, the swimming baths might be shutting down in six months time, which gives you the opportunity to work backwards and set clearly defined deadlines for different aspects of your campaign. Given that most of us have appalling attention spans, the shorter the time period, the better in regards to generating support.

The general rules of community campaigns

› Once you have set the parameters of your campaign, you should look to others in the community to help carry the load. Deciding to run it alone is only sensible if you are a rampant egotist, want to jealously guard the campaign, and have lots of time and resources available. You should look to get a range of people to help and the more diverse the group, the better. By having a good mix of people, you get a range of different opinions which help inform the decision-making, and make it less likely that you will experience 'group-think', the phenomenon where people become scared to speak out in case they are made to look stupid.

› With the parameters set, you must work out a clear action plan, including any engagement with the media, politicians and the public. This plan should also include the phases the campaign will go through, e.g. to begin with letter-writing and responding to formal consultations, but to finish with a march on Downing Street.

› If you are battling for your community, then the same community has the right to expect you to stay engaged with them. This means frequent contact with the people who have sent you letters, emails or just signed a petition. When people feel involved, they tend to stay involved. You should therefore always report back, even if it is via a Facebook campaign page or standard website.

› When the last of the tatty placards have been wiped down and stored in the shed, do take the opportunity to properly evaluate the success or otherwise, of the campaign. Ask yourself what you could have done differently or better if you had a second chance. Doing the same thing over and over again, yet expecting a different outcome is akin to madness. Failure is a form of feedback, so make sure you heed it.

Construct a message grid

Using a message grid is an effective way of making sure your community campaign is properly and professionally planned. A grid is simply a way of outlining the nature of your campaign, and coordinating activity within it. A grid allows you to develop your key messages for each stage of the campaign.

The best way to ensure you begin your campaign with a clear set of messages is to create a message grid for each day/week/month of your campaign. Taking the time to develop a grid for a campaign is the political equivalent of an architect developing a blueprint for an office block.

If you talk to people in your community, define a set of succinct messages and align them to an action, your campaign will be better disciplined and give you the best possible chance of setting the pace. A grid provides a spine to your activities and ensures that your entire team is left in no doubt as to the theme(s) of any given day. Campaigns often fail because the message development process lacks discipline and mistakes are made, therefore risking handing the advantage to your opponents.

Of course, there is a temptation to propel your grid towards the waste paper basket if a sudden event threatens to blow you off course. However, this is still a situation where the grid can help you to recover more quickly from a setback. Even if you make an error the focus remains on the core messages you know play well with your audiences. These core or strategic messages should stay the same throughout, even though the tactical ones can be adapted according to circumstances.

If you do not have much money to spend, hand delivering leaflets with feedback or 'grumble' slips might tease out what the key local issues are. It is also worth keeping an eye on the local and regional papers to see what stories are causing the most concern. Either way, you ideally need this data generated and understood before you hone your message grid.

There are a number of ways of constructing a message grid, but along the left hand side you would usually break down the period of the campaign into time chunks, with the key campaign topics along the top.

Within each box, you should succinctly, in a maximum of one paragraph, outline your candidate's position on said issue, but also align each message with a campaign action. This might mean holding a press conference, organising a placard waving demonstration, or hand delivering some leaflets. You should also include a few lines on why your opponent's arguments are wrong. Hopefully you will not have to use negative campaigning, but it can be very effective if deployed in the right way at the right time.

So the key message is to work out what you want to say, when you want to say it, and put it down on paper. Put the grid on the wall in your study and make sure your supporters have memorised it before the starting pistol is fired. The message grid might just make the difference.

An illustration of what your grid for a post office campaign might look like is on the next page.

Setting the right tone

The best political campaigns are based on inspiring hopes and dreams rather than fears and problems. Martin Luther King Jr did not seal his place in history by proclaiming, 'I have a nightmare', though it is unlikely that your local campaign will get the opportunity to be as inspirational. After all, King was leading the civil rights movement at the height of the social revolution of the 1960s; you will be merely trying to keep a local shop open.

But both styles of campaign do require you to persuade others that you can deliver on your vision and that tangible benefits will follow if they support your campaign. Negative campaigns that exploit dark emotions such as fear or anger can mobilise people initially, but in the long term are not likely to build strong advocates or win the argument.

As well as the right tone, a good campaign also identifies its key messages and does not get diverted by events and attacks from the opposition. That is why a positive message is so much more difficult to attack and it ensures that you ultimately keep the moral high ground.

Campaigns will only succeed if you can make your target audience identify with your issue so make sure you know who they are and research their concerns, values and views on the issue. Using this data, you can then create a clear identity and a memorable message that your community will understand. This might even mean designing logos and creating a catchy slogan that people identify with the campaign. Barack Obama used: 'Yes, we can!'; Tony Blair said: 'Things can only get better.' Yours do not have to be so grand but you get the point. When you have a good slogan or succinct sound bite make sure you include it in each speech you make or press release you send out.

	Week 1 28 Feb–6 Mar	Week 2 7–13 Mar	Week 3 14–20 Mar	Week 4 21–27 Mar	Week 5 28 Mar–3 Apr
Main event	Production of community leaflet and hand delivery to neighbours	Official campaign launch outside of post office threatened with closure	Hand petition to local MP outside of Parliament	Public show of support for campaign via rally	Meeting with postmaster's union to demand counter remains open or replacement site found
Media	Speak to news desk on local paper to inform them of campaign launch on 8 March	Photos of local campaigners, esp. those most affected such as the elderly and full-time mums	Photo of petition being handed to MP in Westminster	News story: campaigners holding mini-rally in town centre	Prominent piece in local paper reflecting importance of meeting
Social media	Set up Facebook campaign page and Twitter feed	Send Twitter messages during course of campaign launch and publish photos online	Ask MP to use his/her own Twitter site to highlight campaign	Use Facebook campaign page to get locals to attend mini-rally	Provide immediate feedback on meeting via Twitter to increase pressure to find a solution
Opinion	Test opinion of community towards the counter closures, esp. elderly and mums. Find out who are willing to appear at campaign launch and sign petition	Collect petition signatures at launch event for the basis of a Westminster photo opportunity with local MP	N/A	Visit ten local businesses to gauge opinion about proposed counter closures. Encourage them to write letters to Post Office Ltd	Use findings of opinion research in meeting with Post Office Ltd

Top down and bottom up

The best pressure to exert on decision-makers is simultaneously from the top down and bottom up. Too many people make the mistake of only focusing a community campaign on the most senior person taking a decision. Of course, it is correct that you need to target the top brass, rather than get bogged down with middle management at the council or hospital trust etc. But your campaign also needs citizens who are willing to act in support. That is why everything you put out during your campaign – leaflets, YouTube videos, letters to the local newspaper – needs to include a 'call to action'. Most people will only do one thing for your campaign, so make sure you have a mobilising and organising strategy.

Set goals and objectives

Your campaign should have very clear objectives or goals. You may have long-term objectives as well as short-term objectives. For example, in a campaign to prevent motorists speeding along your road, your long-term objective might be to persuade the council to introduce speed-bumps. But as that could take many months, even years, to achieve, your short-term objective might be to persuade the local police to deter people from driving too fast.

When you set your objectives, you should keep in mind the following:

› An objective should be measurable – you need to know what success looks like.

› It should have a deadline, otherwise decision-makers will feel no pressure to act quickly. This also helps encourage your supporters to stick with it, as there is a clearly defined timeframe.

› The objective should be stretching, but realistic. For example, you might be successful in keeping the last post office counter in the town open, but less so if you are asking for the other five which had recently closed to all re-open too.

Understand your audiences

As I mentioned previously, there are many ways to do research that will help you to understand what your community thinks about the campaign issue you are engaged with. It is always a mistake for a politician, corporation or individual to assume that they understand public opinion without even bothering to test it.

The Conservative Party disappeared from view for a while following its general election defeat in 1997. This was partly because it made assumptions about the key issues which were at the front of people's minds. They believed that voters cared most about issues related to the European Union. In reality, people cared more about the standard of schools and hospitals, as well as the state of the economy. Yet despite their own opinion polling telling them otherwise, the Conservatives presumed that the polling was wrong, rather than their own message.[10] Needless to say, they continued to lose heavily until they started talking about other issues too.

If you want a campaign to succeed, you need to know what people really think and what they want. Professional focus groups cost a few thousand pounds to run, which is why they are usually only conducted by political parties and corporations. Focus groups are small gatherings of people, perhaps no more than eight, representing one of your target groups, that are brought together for discussion around issues linked to the campaign. You can use them to get an in-depth understanding of attitudes and desires, respond to your message, or test slogans on them. Defining what information you want from the group is key so that the discussion is steered in the right direction. Your participants

10. http://www.telegraph.co.uk/news/uknews/1311801/Hague-exit-leaves-Tories-at-crossroads.html

need to be in an atmosphere that allows them to interact freely with a facilitator.

The facilitator asks some questions related to issues around the campaign and ensures that everyone participates in the discussion and is open about their attitudes and feelings. Professional focus groups are usually divided according to age, gender, race, income levels, geographic location and other categories so that the perspective of each group can be analysed separately. People are then recruited for these different categories of groups.

The discussions from the focus groups are analysed and used to refine your campaign message to make sure that your target group will respond. Focus groups are only useful when there are very specific questions that need to be checked. For example the group could discuss their response to a particular advert that you want to run for your campaign.

You can undertake a similar exercise when planning your own campaign. You can run focus groups by yourself with sufficient preparation. This might mean doing a rough and ready focus group in the community, handpicking a group of people you know represent different parts of the community and inviting them round to your house, or a neutral venue, and chatting through what they really think about the issue you are campaigning on. So if your local nursery is threatened with closure, you need to know if the majority view amongst parents is in favour of moving to a different venue, or fighting to retain the existing site.

The other often overlooked resource is other people's polling. Lots of major research organisations conduct surveys as part of their marketing efforts. By getting a poll published in a major national newspaper they are potentially attracting companies to also use their services. I have listed a range of top pollsters and their website addresses in the Resources section later in the book, but you can find a whole wealth of information which might be relevant to you too. Very few organisations can afford to do the type of research that involves interviewing thousands of people. Try to find out whether any surveys have been done about the issue that you are campaigning on, and if possible get the result analysis from the people who did the survey. For example, post office closures are taking place up and down the country so it is both a local and national issue. Therefore you can use some of the national findings and adapt them to your own patch.

Lastly, you can undertake your own surveys too, simply by adding a 'grumble slip' or feedback box in your leaflets. This encourages people to think about the issues which most concern them in the local area. Or you can ask your own multiple choice questions about the specific issue you are campaigning on, such as the preferred location of a new community facility. It is quite simple to do your own survey. If you want it to be reliable, choosing your sample (namely, a small representation of the total group of people in your community) is very important. Make sure your sample is big enough because if it is too small the results will not be reliable.

Your sample must be representative. Try to find out how many people live in the area in terms of the number of men and women, different age groups, different income groups, different educational level and different ethnic/language/religious groups. You can get this information from the census results in your area. Once you know who lives in the area you must make sure your sample has the right percentage of each group so that it can be representative. For example if 5 per cent of the people in your area are unemployed people between the ages of 18–25, 5 per cent of your sample should be comprised of such people.

Your sample should also aim to be random. This means that you cannot choose which people you interview but you must use a system that leaves the choice to chance. Avoid interviewing people you know just because it is more comfortable.

Try not to put too many questions in the survey and make sure they are as clear and simple as possible. Even your elderly grandmother should be able to fully understand what is being asked. Also try to set questions in such a way that they can be answered with 'yes', 'no' or 'don't know'.

Get out the vote

Armed with data about how local people think on a given issue, your mobilising strategy will aim to reach the broad public, to get your message to them and to generate support. Political parties talk about the importance of the GOTV operation (Get Out The Vote), namely that although people might have pledged support, you also need them to act upon it. Most of your campaign budget and human resources should be spent on this part of the campaign. Mobilisation is hard work and it is tempting to spend more on media and do less direct contact and outreach work. Remember that it is easier to change people and to get them involved in your campaign if you are interacting and engaging with them directly.

Your mobilisation strategy depends on the nature and target of your campaign and you should spend some time on careful planning. It should focus on the following:

› Identify where your target audiences are located.

› Decide which methods will be most effective to get to them and then tailor messages to passive and active supporters.

› Get key individuals in the community to publicly back you – for example local personalities, popular people and organisations' leaders.

› Do not create a talking shop. Organise activities that will mobilise and involve people.

› Ensure you regularly refer to the message grid to work out the phases of your campaign and when the campaign will peak.

Assess your own team

You need a well-oiled machine to run a good community campaign, so it is important for you to analyse what strengths exist within your team. This exercise must be done collectively so that everyone contributes and understands the reasons for the analysis.

Some of your strengths could be people who have experience within the community, are hard working and have a good understanding of the campaign issues. On the other hand you may have a number of weaknesses which you need to be aware of and, if possible, deal with them before starting on the campaign. These could be weaknesses like not having enough volunteers, lack of resources or lack of support from influential people.

This analysis will help you to build on, and use, your strengths to make the campaign more effective. It will also help you to work out how to deal with some of your weaknesses and overcome them. You must recognise that there are weaknesses which you may not be able to do anything about.

Opportunities and threats

Strengths and weaknesses are mainly about your team and your internal issues. Opportunities and threats relate much more to external issues based in the community or broader environment within which you will run your campaign. You need to analyse beforehand what these opportunities and threats are so that you can use the opportunities and try to neutralise or deal with the threats.

An analysis of opportunities means knowing what issues – like the mood of the community, upcoming events and available resources – can help your campaign and move it forward. In an election campaign some opportunities could be that a massive new housing project is about to be opened and you can use that event to gain some political support. Threats are the opposite of opportunities and will have a negative effect on your campaign. Examples could be that the opposition is spreading misinformation or that you have to deal with hostile newspaper coverage. Both these could lead to less support for your activities, so you will need to deal with these issues strategically, speedily and decisively.

Develop a campaign strategy

Once you have done your research and analysis you then have to develop clear communications, and organising and training strategies. Elements of your communication strategy should be the following:

› Identify the key message themes that you want to communicate to your target audience. Develop a communications strategy to get your message across to the audience.
› Develop a slogan and a media design identity like a logo.
› Draw up media plans with budget and time frames.
› Develop a public relations plan.
› Develop a campaign and training strategy amongst the key players in your organisation that focuses on reaching and mobilising your target audience

Message themes

Message themes are the key things that you want people to know and agree with. A message is not the same as a slogan. A slogan is usually a few words that sum up the message. Message themes can be a few sentences that explain your main ideas. These themes should be the basis of all communications like posters, pamphlets, speeches, interviews, submissions and petitions.

Everyone involved in the campaign should understand the message and stay on it – one spokesperson contradicting your message on TV or radio can ruin a campaign.

An example of a slogan for a campaign against the closure of a local post office might be: 'Don't K.O. the P.O. – save the local post office.'

The message themes for the campaign would be:

> The post office is more than a shop, it is a meeting place for the community.
> It is especially important for the elderly and stay-at-home parents.
> The alternative site is over two miles away and difficult to reach.
> The other site will only get busier, leading to longer queues.
> Post Office Ltd has not provided sufficient incentives to keep the counter open.

As you can see, these are a range of messages, both positive and negative but all motivating people to act. They are so simple that they can be used in a range of campaign scenarios and are easily deployed as a sound bite for the local newspaper or television station. They can also be used in leaflets, letters, Facebook pages, Twitter messages and even public debates.

When I stood successfully as a candidate in the local elections, I inherited leaflets which consisted of four, text heavy, pages which were sent out in the run-up to polling day. It was typical to have a few grainy photos on the front, surrounded by dense, complex wording. Just as the messages themes for the post office campaign, I stripped all of that down to its core. The new two-sided version consisted of a large photo of me doing something active in the community, with a strong, emboldened headline and punchy text which could be understood by almost any reader. The time between someone picking up a leaflet from the door mat to placing it into their bin is less than ten seconds. It is vital to be clear and succinct in your messaging and campaign communications.

Media plan
A media plan should be developed according to the phases of your campaign – work out when you will need most public-

ity and how you will get it. Remember to strategise how to get free publicity through the press, radio and TV. Activities could include building good relationships with the media, holding briefing sessions, issuing press statements, organising and publicising newsworthy events, and photo opportunities.

Your budget and the level of contacts you have developed will determine how much media you can produce yourself. The media plan should have clear time frames and deadlines and for each part of the plan you must work out the cost and make sure you have the money to pay for it. But the better the relationship you build with your local and regional media, the more likely it is that coverage can be attained for little or no money.

Why 'local' matters

Although I have run high profile campaigns in London and Brussels, nothing quite matches the hustle and bustle of a good local campaign. The smaller the town or village, the more controversial it is to close a post office counter, village pub or attempt to build a new housing development. If you live in the centre of bustling London or Manchester, change is an accepted part of life. If you live in Chipping Sodbury or a small Surrey hamlet, change is often a swear word. But local community campaigns can be very empowering and bring neighbourhoods closer together.

At the same time that globalisation has spread, and the balance of world power begins to slowly shift to the East, politics in the UK has become increasingly influenced by a move toward localism. Much of this was driven by the Liberal Democrats who built their power base in what had threatened to become a two-party state. They have long understood the attractiveness to voters of more attentive and community-focused political action. This has fundamentally changed our expectations of what a constituency MP should be. I suspect that it will not be at the top of your bedtime reading list but a Liberal (before they merged with the SDP) activist Bernard Greaves wrote a pamphlet, with Gordon Lishman, called *The Theory and Practice of Community Politics* just around the time that Thatcher became Prime Minister. This publication was the template for a new insurgency style of politics, which was developed by the Liberal Democrats' elections chief Lord Rennard to devastating effect in parliamentary by-elections.

The principles are quite clear. If you grew up in Rochdale, you are more likely to care about its future and understand its past. You will know the differences between electoral wards. You will know what local buildings, green spaces and services are especially important to the community. Even when you make mistakes, at least it will be on the basis of poor judgement rather than not understanding the area. The genius of the Liberal Democrat approach was therefore to take on the major parties by working harder than them in the community. Road resurfaced? No problem. Streetlight fixed? Leave it to us. This type of activity means more to local people than grand speeches on national issues because it makes a real and tangible difference. It also means the local campaigner rises above the party political fray and becomes known by their personal 'brand', i.e. 'I would usually vote Conservative but Joe Bloggs works so hard that I'm going to give him my vote instead.'

This localised approach to politics is attractive because there are so many aspects to our daily interaction with government, both local and national, which are unsatisfactory. But most of us waste time and energy grumbling to one another or simply throw our hands up and accept the status quo. It is this 'cannot be bothered' response which has allowed government to get away with offering second-rate services despite taking more and more of our money. If you buy a new car and find it has a big dent in it when it arrives on the forecourt you would not dream of simply shrugging your shoulders and accepting it. You would demand a replacement or a refund. Yet when your bins are not collected, more houses are crammed into your already overloaded community, the local hospital is unclean, or your children leave school unable to read and write properly, many of us just quietly accept it.

Case study: Save our hospital

Although the rest of my examples are real-life experiences, let us take some of the key lessons and test them on a typical community campaign, such as the closure of the local Accident and Emergency unit (A&E).

Scenario: The local A&E service is being threatened with closure in an attempt to save money. Little to no information is being provided at this stage with only leaked information trickling into the public domain. Local people, who rely on this crucial service, are anxious about what this means for them and their families, especially if they have to start travelling to the nearest A&E, an additional twenty-minute drive away.

Stage 1: The first step is to bring together the various strands of the campaign into a cohesive centre. Find out who the decision-makers and influencers are (i.e., people who shape the way decision-makers think) and put them onto a list. The list will probably consist of:

- The Chief Executive of the local NHS Trust
- Secretary of State for Health
- Shadow Secretary of State for Health
- The constituency MP
- County councillor (x1)
- District/borough councillor(s) (usually x3)
- Editor/senior reporter – local newspapers
- Contact details for local/regional TV channels

With this list, you then need to identify what the 'pressure points' are. They are likely to be as follows:

Local MP: they will see this issue as both a threat and an opportunity. On the one hand, it may be that their own party is in government, therefore there is an element of collective responsibility. If they are seen to be too outspoken, the party whips (those who are charged with keeping discipline to ensure the government's business progresses) will haul them into their parliamentary offices and 'gently' remind the MP that being in government means often supporting tough decisions for the greater good of the country. However, as a representative of a constituency, it would be political suicide to not at least show sympathy to the cause. Even better, if the MP finds a way to 'own' this issue in the local community, it could play a significant role in safeguarding their seat at the next election. Photos of an MP in action always look good on glossy constituency leaflets.

Councillor: the electoral considerations are still there, just not as significant, as it tends not to be a full-time job. Local councillors may not have health services directly under their control, but residents/voters will not understand the distinction. So being part of such a campaign can only bring benefits to their own profile. They will want to be on the right side of the debate, and they have no worries about a threatening visit from the whip.

Trust chief executives: they have the unenviable task of seeing through the closure of the A&E whether they agree with it or not. The Department of Health will be looking for cost-cutting measures and if the A&E service is considered to be underused, it makes the pressure even greater. So the chief executive will be looking to please the diametrically opposed audiences, namely the health ministry on the one hand and his/her staff at the hospital on the other. They will need to handle the claims that jobs will be on the line, and that the safety of local people will be compromised. They will also be thinking about their own careers – namely, if this planned closure is botched, will they get another major job in the future? It is this pressure point you will need to exploit.

Party spokespeople: the government has a Secretary of State for Health. Whoever is in opposition at the time will have a 'shadow' for that role, with the job of holding the government to account. It is highly likely that the person in charge of taking health decisions has little practical experience of the health service. Formerly working as a doctor, nurse, or surgeon is certainly a rarity for a senior health minister. Health is one of the biggest jobs in government, but someone in that role will hope that it is not the pinnacle of their political career. They will have an eye on the bigger jobs such as Foreign Secretary, Chancellor of the Exchequer or perhaps even Prime Minister. So they are all too aware that one false move, perhaps being identified as the cruel axe man of the local A&E, could help to spell the end of their steady progress to the top. That is the pressure point.

Opposition parties: they will simply be desperate to get noticed. Opposing the decision to close the A&E is a total no-brainer, and every shadow health secretary will claim that all emergency health services would be safe under their management, regardless of how often it is used or how much money needs to be saved in the NHS budget. The pressure point here is that they need publicity and are desperate to be noticed by anybody at all.

Local media: they will be keen to find something interesting to write about, which could rise above the mundane stuff they are stuck with most weeks. This story will be manna from heaven, with lots of great photos on the front pages of placard-wielding pensioners, mums, and children which in turn sells newspapers. In a brief stint on a local newspaper I once questioned why we needed a photo of an entire under-14's hockey team in the main edition. The editor pulled me to one side and told me to count the number of people in the photo. There were sixteen teenagers in total looking back at me. He then reminded me that each of these teenagers have at least ten family and friends who will be looking out for it, leading to potentially another 160 copies of the paper being sold. That is why local papers are so packed with photos of seemingly uninteresting events: it drives sales. The pressure point, therefore, is to help a journalist to sell newspapers.

Armed with your list of local interested parties and their pressure points, you need to plan what you hope the campaign will look like once fully underway. The first step is to contact your local MP as I explained in the first chapter (by email, letter or telephone) and let them know that you intend to undertake a campaign to save the A&E. You want their support. Subtle pressure can also be executed by explaining that you also intend to contact the local media.

As a fictitious campaign, I cannot provide this case study with a real ending. But community groups throughout Britain have managed to wage similar campaigns against hospital closures, such as Save Kidderminster Hospital. Although the Accident and Emergency facilities were closed before he was elected, the campaign led to the election of its spokesman, Dr Richard Taylor. Some functions of the hospital's A&E unit have been restored, although the campaign continues.

Case study: The post office

Let me now outline a real-life campaign which I succeeded in running. Post offices have been steadily closing over the past fifteen years as it becomes increasingly uneconomic to have so many in operation. More than nine out of every ten of us visit a post office branch each year[11] and for many people they are not simply a commercial enterprise. Post offices in many towns or villages are particularly a lifeline to the elderly and to stay-at-home parents. If you take the local branch away, it means long drives to the nearest large town just to send off a package. In my town, the 'rationalisation' process was especially ruthless with four out of five post offices closing in the town in just a couple of years. This meant that the only remaining counter would be in the local Safeway supermarket, with queues often snaking outside.

But just when it appeared that it could not get worse, it became clear that the supermarket giant Morrisons was

11. http://www.postoffice.co.uk/portal/po/content2?catId=20000192&media Id=57600693

about to acquire Safeway. This was bad news because the new owners had a clear corporate policy not to permit post office counters in their stores. So it suddenly became a race against time to find an alternative provider before the final axe fell. The alternative was to travel to a neighbouring town and use a post office in the centre which was already at full capacity. The prospect of going from five post offices to zero in the space of twelve months was unthinkable, and therefore it was necessary to launch an immediate campaign.

Before the campaign was fully underway, I did some personal research by visiting local businesses and neighbours to ascertain local opinion on the closures. After all, what is the point of a community campaign that the community itself does not support? The overwhelming view was that the closure of post office counters in the town had been costly to local shopkeepers, many of whom rely on postal services to send products to customers. Travelling to a busier branch two or three miles away meant being longer away from the shop, and therefore had a significant financial impact. My neighbours had also told me that they would support the campaign in any way possible, which gave me the relevant information to populate a message grid. This discipline would prove useful as the campaign progressed.

There were six stages to the campaign, creating a snowstorm effect. The aim was to overwhelm the post office with a relentless flow of publicity and local activism. Let us look at each stage to draw out why they were effective in forcing change.

> **Stage 1**: I launched a petition, not because I believe that they are usually worth spending too much time on, but because of the publicity opportunity it presented on this particular occasion. Even without a single signatory on the sheet, this immediately created a story and so I called the local newspaper and told them that I was starting this campaign, and where I hoped it would end up.

Sad to say, but it was probably one of the most interesting stories that had come across their desks for a number of weeks. The story also provided my telephone number and email address to encourage interested local people to find out more. The very next day after publication I got a call from a couple in the town who were planning to launch a local shopping reward scheme, and were willing to help publicise my campaign too.

> **Stage 2:** I designed a leaflet, admittedly with the help of a friend, which featured a large headline 'Don't K.O. the P.O.' As I was also planning to run as a council candidate in the next set of local elections, I had the help of some local activists who helped me to deliver to all the hundreds of homes in my 'ward'. But on a smaller scale it is very easy for you to print off 100 or so leaflets using your standard home equipment, or photocopy at the local newsagents, and hand deliver to your neighbours.

> **Stage 3:** In order to keep a high profile on the campaign, I wrote a letter to Patricia Hewitt, the then Secretary of State for Trade and Industry (now known as Business, Innovation and Skills). I called on her to keep the last remaining post office counter open in the town, and informed her that we would be fighting tooth and nail until we got what we want. Now, I was fully aware that a) any response would not be written by the minister herself, but rather using a standard template, b) the response would be anodyne and c) it would take about two months to arrive. I can confirm that all of my predictions came true. But that misses the point. To most readers of the local newspaper, the idea that someone in the community would have the temerity to write to a member of the Cabinet was enough to make it newsworthy, which led to an increase in requests for the petition and a willingness of ordinary people to lobby the Post Office.

› **Stage 4**: Petitions as part of a formal response to a consultation are not that useful. However, we managed to collect just over 250 signatures from local residents. I cut each of the signature boxes out, and spaced them out on a number of pages to create the impression of an overwhelming response. With this ready to go, I then telephoned my Member of Parliament and requested a photo opportunity with him outside of St Stephen's entrance at the House of Commons. MPs love to be provided with a free opportunity to get their faces in the local paper, especially when they are seen to be supporting a community campaign. Having the MP on board also meant that his sway with the local press would guarantee coverage the following week. Even better, the MP was heading into the Chamber to speak in a debate about this very subject and put on the record that he had received a petition. In fact we got a two page broadsheet-sized story in the big regional newspaper, complete with colour photos of the petition being handed over. Not bad for just 250 signatures.

› **Stage 5**: Along similar lines to the letter to the DTI, I noticed that there was also going to be a parliamentary select committee inquiry into the ongoing programme of post office closures. Utterly shamelessly, I decided to submit written evidence (usually a few pages expressing a view on the subject in question) to the committee. Once again, I publicised this fact with the local papers who were only too happy to cover it. Was I called up to appear before the committee? Of course not. But I made the effort and made sure everyone in the locality also knew I had. It was all part of keeping the momentum in the campaign.

› **Stage 6**: Using the influence of my local MP, I also engineered a meeting with the general manager of the post office urban network in order to push for a greater effort to find a new location for the threatened supermarket post office counter. The meeting was more than a little heated, but the representative was left in little doubt at the importance of finding a solution. This meeting was then reported in the local paper, keeping the campaign's profile high.

So was all of this effort worthwhile? Yes. Victory was secured soon after the meeting with the Post Office's representative when it was announced that a brand new four-counter facility was being opened in a nearby newsagent right in the heart of the community. It meant that this vital service was secured in the community by a smart local businessman who saw a benefit in taking up the challenge.

Our MP told the local paper 'I am grateful to all of those who signed petitions, wrote letters, and in any way helped local councillors and myself put pressure on the Post Office to keep a proper facility open.'

What I found especially heartening following the success was the response from those who had signed the petition and written letters of support. They were genuinely surprised that something they had supported in their community actually made a difference, because so often we support campaigns and respond to consultations only to find that we have still been ignored.

There are a range of lessons to learn from the post office campaign, namely:

> **Set a clear objective** and set of strategies which everyone taking part fully understands. The objective in this instance was to keep the last post office counter open; the strategy was to use relentless publicity to pressurise the Post Office Ltd to find an alternative site.

> Harness (where possible) the **emotion** of the community issue on which you are campaigning, and link the

planned closure or development to a tangible impact on 'real' people. For example, the post office counter is a 'lifeline to the elderly' and the local school playing field is not just a patch of grass but a 'vital recreation space for our children'.

› Whatever you do, plot a way to maintain **momentum** throughout your campaign. Do not allow quiet periods where your issue is not being talked about. Decision-makers do not take decisions unless they are pressured to do so.

› Help your supporters feel included in the campaign by providing them with **regular updates**. Give them evidence that it was worth bothering to write a letter or turn out on a rainy Saturday afternoon to hold a placard.

› Do not be afraid to **think outside of the proverbial box**. Making a submission to a major parliamentary select committee or writing to a member of the Cabinet might seem scary but it will set you apart and make people sit up and take notice.

Case study: The mobile phone mast

Let us be completely honest about our hypocrisy when it comes to mobile phones. There are very few of us left who do not own one; in fact, 15 per cent of UK households have no fixed land line[12]. In order to use a mobile, you also need a signal generated by a mast. We all know that irritation when you are on an important call and you drive through an area which has barely any coverage. But try to put a mobile phone mast near to where we live and we lose our minds in fear and panic. Despite scare stories and twenty years of research, we have to accept that there is still no evidence whatsoever that those masts create health problems.

12. http://news.bbc.co.uk/1/hi/8355504.stm

That said, masts are ugly, intrusive and blight properties and neighbourhoods, and there are some places which are more sensible than others to put them. Mobile phone companies adopt a strategy which makes perfect commercial sense, but can lead to terrible impacts on a community. They tend to put in mass applications for new masts in any given area, in the hope that one or two of the masts will make it through. It also occupies and ties up community groups who then find it more difficult to table objections to multiple sites.

On one occasion I discovered that a 40 foot mobile phone mast was being planned for the end of my road. Despite the natural NIMBY reaction which we all initially have, I would not have opposed it had it been planned to go somewhere sensible. At the bottom of my road also happened to be a church which doubled up as a children's crèche during the day. So we were to have a 40 foot mast on the main road, right outside a place of worship which also housed young children. At best it was insensitive and inappropriate.

Leaping into action, I started the process of informing my neighbours and other locally affected roads. Although I did take round a petition, the priority had to be to get people motivated to individually write to the mobile phone company, plus the local planning officials at the council who would process the application. It is important to remember planning officers are there to ensure that the application meets certain criteria, rather than whether they like the proposed development or not. Simply saying no is not an option because any such decision can then be legally challenged, costing the local taxpayer money as well as still being lumbered with the development.

One Saturday morning I gathered up a number of other local residents, especially those with children, and invited the local paper to come down and take a photo. For maximum impact, the children were snapped at the front of the church, looking forlorn and sad. This gave the campaign a human face. To position a community campaign as David vs

Goliath, creating a diametric opposition, makes the story as interesting as possible to the local media.

With the photographer snapping away, I knew we would get good coverage, and a colour photo and accompanying story duly appeared. In order to really have an impact and influence, people agreed to write personally (not with template letters) to the planning team but also the specific mobile phone company. It is a crude process but the only way to really get what you want in this instance is to project strength. The aim was to make putting a mobile phone mast on this site more trouble than it was worth, and this often works because the longer a planning application takes, the more expensive it becomes for a developer.

We achieved victory a few weeks later when the mobile phone operator threw in the towel and accepted defeat. They did get another mast approved later that year but it was set hundreds of meters away from the local housing and the church, and even had to be disguised as a tree in order to proceed. So our properties escaped the visual blight, the church could continue unimpeded and people still got improved phone coverage.

Why did this work?

> **Do not waste time** on making arguments which cannot be reasonably supported by hard evidence. You might believe that mobile phone masts can be linked to cancer, but tens of millions of pounds of independent scientific research suggests otherwise. Focus on what you can prove – namely, that a mast would be inappropriately placed, with an impact on 'visual amenity', for example.

> **Find the human story** in the campaign – in this instance, the impact on church-goers (with its implied religious overtones), and the disruption to the children's crèche.

> **Create a diametric opposition** – good versus evil might be stretching it a little far, but you get my point. Having

clear sides means people have to choose which one they are on. In a community campaign it will almost certainly be yours.

> Make sure that **developing on your road becomes more trouble than it is worth**. This means publicity, harnessing local support and peppering the company with letters of objection.

Conclusion

Of all the ways you can campaign, nothing is as satisfying as winning in your community. Success does not just transform your life, but the lives of many other people in your area. It bonds neighbours together and creates a sense of pride in your collective achievements. And there is no better time to be actively engaged in this type of activity, with the coalition government committed to the empowering of local communities by giving them increased rights and responsibilities.

This chapter should have provided you with a clearer idea of the preparations you need to make in order to succeed. Campaigns do not require professionals to run them. But they do need proper planning and coordination. There is still a considerable gap between what communities would like to achieve and the skills required to win. This is even more important with the advent of modern campaigning and communications techniques, which are evolving at a much quicker pace.

Chapter 6: The nuts and bolts of the modern campaign

The advent of the internet has not only revolutionised the way we access services and buy products, but also the way we engage with the political process. Whereas previously people had to fill out forms, write letters, sign petitions and attend public meetings in order to engage, they can now participate at the click of a button. Social networks have become almost as important as human contact in demonstrating our feelings towards a whole range of policy issues, both locally and nationally. Using the internet we can talk to government at any time of the day. Whether they are listening is another matter, but the principle remains the same.

Keeping abreast of the dominant new ways to engage is worthwhile to ensure that you are maximising your efforts to get what you want, and I have identified some of the key aspects.

Fundraising

As a mere volunteer for a community campaign, most of what you can offer is your spare time. This will usually be time outside of your day-to-day responsibilities as an employee or as a housewife/househusband. Using your time wisely and working hard is usually enough to deliver success. However, there may be times when your community campaign requires financial support too, especially if you are up against a powerful company or individual. If a company plans to put a new waste incinerator near to your house, they will be backed with serious financial muscle.

In order to be able to compete in this kind of battle, you could find the need to raise significant sums of money. This money would be spent on paying for professional lobbying support, lawyers, printing leaflets, publicity stunts etc. The anti-airport expansion lobby or those opposed to the new proposal to build a high speed rail line between London and Birmingham have felt it necessary to professionalise their campaigns. This is because the issues affect lots of communities, and the developments have had government support. But because of their slick operation, both campaigns have been able to punch well above their weight.

Many people in politics have tried to mimic the success of Barack Obama in his remarkable journey from freshman senator to leader of the free world. But almost all have failed. Gordon Brown and David Cameron both pinched his language and soaring rhetoric at various times during the past two years, but it fell flat. The reason is that Obama represented something different, new, radical, and genuine change; Brown and Cameron did no such thing.

But what Obama did introduce, which can be replicated to some degree, is the remarkable story of how he managed to raise more money than Hilary Clinton, arguably the most powerful woman in the world, back in 2008. Clinton knew every major donor in the Democratic Party. Her husband (and former President) Bill already had a loyal fan base she could tap into and as she was an inevitable winner of the next election, it was not difficult to raise funds. After all, everyone wants to be able to say that they were in early with the next President. Obama, on the other hand, was still agonising over whether he was ready to run at all. Given his youthful appearance and the weight of history he would have to overcome, the big temptation was for him to get behind Hilary and build his profile up during the course of the next eight years.

When he did decide to run, there were some people willing to provide financial support, but not nearly enough. So his team started to focus on his key strengths, namely that he was different, a break from the past. Small donations started to trickle in, $10 here, $20 there, from ordinary people who wanted to play a role in getting Obama to the White House. This was extraordinarily successful, so much so that in one single month (February 2008), Obama managed to raise around $55 million for his campaign.

The fact that these small sums of money were trickling in was not only financially significant for his campaign, but because it created a network of grass roots supporters who would feel some sense of ownership of a national campaign for the White House. It was no longer multimillionaire industrialists and movie stars who dictated who won but ordinary folk too.

You might justifiably be asking what the relevance is of Obama's multimillion dollar presidential campaign and your local community campaign to save a school playing field or to see off a high speed rail line. It shows that long lasting grass roots campaigns are successful not just because of ideas, fancy leaflets or gimmicks, but because of people, lots of people, wanting something to happen. You don't even need to be in the majority, just part of a large enough, and vocal enough, group that collectively makes decision-makers sit up and take notice.

Although I showed in the first section of this book that asserting your rights as an individual can be successful, this obviously has limitations when you are dealing with a bigger community issue. If you are the only person who is complaining that a school is being closed, then why should anyone take time to listen to you? The simple answer is that no one will. But a campaign which has 200 people outside of the school with placards, attracting the attention of the local media, poses an immediate threat to the people that matter. You are now presenting a problem that cannot be ignored, even if they do not initially intend to give you what you want.

One of the very clever ways in which Obama managed to develop such an extraordinary depth of active supporters was by agreeing to speak at fundraising events for fellow Democrats seeking election, in return for getting a download of all of the contact details of the supporters invited to the fundraiser. This data could then be used to generate invaluable lists of potential donors and activists. No one else was doing this.

In a similar way, your community campaign should harness ways to create and collate lists of supporters and sympathisers. That might be via a Facebook page, Twitter, or perhaps simple contact sheets on the bottom of leaflets. Most people who take the time to sign up to a web-based supporters page, or fill out a form and return it to you, are likely to be willing to go even further. You should never be embarrassed to ask supporters on your list to go that extra mile for you in your community campaign. The worst they can say is no, and the reality is that they rarely refuse to help, not least because people tend to be quite vain and enjoy being 'especially selected' to help.

Of course, Obama's campaign was very special. Even the best campaigning tools in the world could not have helped George W. Bush win again had he been permitted to. And the success of these methods in your community will depend greatly on the type of thing that you are campaigning for. Let's say you are trying to protect a special needs school from closure or a cancer unit at the local hospital. It is highly unlikely that you will meet anyone who considers these campaigns not to be worthwhile. This means that generating lists of advocates and active supporters is not going to be too hard. But if your campaign is to build a local waste incinerator near to a school, then even the smartest techniques are not going to help you.

Global campaigns

Participating in global campaigns is in many ways much less satisfying than those taking place in your local area or in the region. By definition, a global campaign involves many people in a number of other countries on an issue which affects the whole of, or a region of, the world. So it is less tangible for you as a campaigner to be involved in. However, like all good projects, a global campaign can be 'chunked down', which simply means that you might be the lead person in your town for a campaign which is global. For example, you might be the coordinator of the Friends of the Earth for the Croydon branch, and therefore have the ability to take decisions on how the campaigns run locally whilst ultimately reporting into a global network. It also means you can find ways of highlighting the things you believe in at a local level and make your politicians accountable.

Facebook campaigns

Unless you have been living on a remote island with no access to civilisation, you will be aware of a social networking site called Facebook. Originally designed as a tool for university students in the United States, Facebook has grown into an international phenomenon with currently over 500 million users. In principle, it is simply a web page with your photograph, some personal details and a group of friends who have agreed to link with you in cyberspace.

For most people, that is the limit of their relationship with this website, along with checking up on ex-girl and boyfriends. But it does provide campaigning opportunities too, which are worth considering. The most obvious way is to create a campaign linked to your own Facebook page. You can invite your friends to join the group in a 'closed' site, i.e. where every prospective member has to ask your permission before they join. The upside of this approach is you can fully control who joins, who sees the information you are sharing, and be able to prevent potential troublemakers from joining. The big downside is that the group is too small, and is unlikely to get to the sort of numbers that might make a difference in a campaign.

Ultimately it depends on the purpose of the campaign page. If it is designed to keep 20–30 people who live in your local community updated, then a closed site is probably best. But an 'open' site, where any Facebook user can join, is definitely best if you are trying to disseminate information to the maximum number of people. Try not to add too much content as really the page should be for people who 'like' the page to interact and to form a community around it, and of course for you to raise awareness about your activities. Facebook pages also allow the use of a 'wall', which means that members can post comments on any subject, which you can reply to, and helps to encourage feedback on the progress of your campaign. Although the numbers of people who sign a petition is relatively meaningless, unless you get a million to do so, the beauty of Facebook campaign pages is the ability to get large numbers of people to do something for your campaign. This is why your cause needs to have a call to action.

Twitter campaigns

If you have only recently joined Facebook, then you might feel that another social networking site, Twitter, is a step too far. Whereas Facebook allows the user to post up lots of photos and have lengthy debates via 'wall' posts, Twitter works in a different but ingenious way. Using only 140 characters or less you post a short item of information. It is similar to a 'status update' on Facebook. Some people use Twitter to communicate in real time with friends, others to inform people that they are heading off to the cinema, or are sat next to a minor celebrity on the train. But in campaign terms, it is most useful for information gathering and sharing.

For example, if you are fighting the closure of a post office, you might create a username such as '@DontKOPO' (i.e. Don't K.O. the P.O.) which could exist alongside your own personal Twitter identity. Using this identity, you can post the campaign latest in your area, and advertise this information source in your local newspaper or via a newsletter. Twitter also allows you to include 'links' in your postings, so you can circulate articles which are interesting to you and/or relevant to the campaign. If your information is interesting enough to others, someone may 'retweet' it, thus circulating it to all their followers too. This can rapidly increase the number of followers to your own site.

Like Facebook, Twitter allows you to either have a closed or open site. The former means someone will need your permission before they can follow your tweets, and the latter means anyone can. My view is to go for 'open' in any campaigning site but just be careful that you do not post anything on the way home from the pub, as it could be a recipe for disaster.

Doing radio

The good news about doing radio is people cannot see you. The bad news is that they will hear you, and judging your tone of voice and the right message is still extremely important. It is helpful to consider how you feel when you are listening to a radio programme and someone starts blathering on. You just wish they would get to the point, which is why you need to have your clear, succinct messages ready and memorised before you get into the studio.

Being on TV for the first time can throw you because you never quite know how you will respond to having a camera staring blankly at you. Being on radio can also be disorientating as you will be led into a small studio with lots of flashing lights and buttons, where a pair of headphones are slapped on you. What is helpful about radio is your ability to bring a note of what you need to say as a safety blanket. Just do not rustle the paper or your audience will also know what you are up to. Radio interviews tend to be short and sharp, especially if it is a news item. In fact, you might only get ten seconds or less to comment. But if you have a clear message, this should be no problem.

Doing TV

Although most campaigns in your community will attract no media attention beyond a small story in the local newspaper, you could feasibly find yourself being asked to appear on television. Very few mediums create such panic in inexperienced campaigners. This is because television reveals all: your facial expression, parts of your body you do not like and your tone of voice.

› The most important thing with any media interview is to learn how to be succinct, delivering clear, concise messages that will resonate with your intended audiences. Take your key campaign aims and boil them down into something which resembles a sound bite.

› Before you agree to be filmed, you need to ensure you understand what the broadcast journalist is seeking from you.

› Consider an appropriate setting for your interview. For example, if you are campaigning in favour of a school or hospital, then use the building as a backdrop. It ensures that anyone quickly glancing at the screen understands the context of your interview.

› Consider the clothes you wear. Bright colours do not tend to look good on television and can be distracting to the viewer. Try to present a smart appearance even if you are wearing casual clothing.

› Think about your body language. Are you saying one thing verbally, but indicating another by your facial expressions? Practise your sound bites in front of a friend, or even a mirror, to strike the right balance.

Public speaking

Do not be frightened but it is possible that your local campaign might make you a minor star in the eyes of the media or politicians, in which case you may find yourself speaking at a conference or press conference. In many ways, this simply requires the same skills as highlighted in the sections on radio and television.

› Find a suitable venue or pick an appropriate conference – do not be afraid to be fussy.

› Careful management of the invite list. You will want to ensure your supporters are present and any opposition is kept away.

› Be very clear what the key message that you want to get across is. Can you sum it up in thirty seconds? You will need to learn the lines off by heart but keep a paper copy to hand as a safety net in case the moment overwhelms you.

› If you are not a confident writer, you will need some support. See who else in the campaign team might be able to assist. If not, how about a friend, a family member or a work colleague? You really need someone to help sense-check your material.

› If the event is really high profile and important you might want to seek professional help. However, you need to be aware that seeking external help can be expensive and should be a last resort if you are not independently wealthy.

› If you are invited to a political party conference to speak, it may appear to be intimidating but lots of other delegates will also be inexperienced. If you have a good story to tell, the audience will want you to succeed. It is also in the interests of the event organisers to ensure that you have all the assistance you need to get it right and survive the experience.

Local newspapers

Throughout my time at school and college, I wanted to be a journalist. I could not imagine a more exciting, dynamic and fulfilling career. When I was offered the opportunity to go and work for my local newspaper, the *Eastbourne Herald*, at the age of seventeen, I expected the job to be full of thrilling exposés, written by a band of men and women in the mould of Woodward and Bernstein (the investigative journalists who uncovered the scandal which led to the resignation of President Nixon in the 1970s). The office, unfortunately, was less Watergate and more waterlogged.

Joking aside, working on a local newspaper is a far from thrilling experience. Once every decade or so, something interesting might happen, such as a major robbery, murder or perhaps the face of Noel Edmonds appearing on a poppadum. Most of the news tends to be stories of church fêtes, jumble sales, and local sporting encounters. So if you have a campaign to share with the paper, they will be very happy indeed to hear from you. My tale about my pregnant wife finding glass in her pizza was a whole half-page of a broadsheet-sized paper; my post office campaign included a double-page spread with colour photos; a campaign to help save my son's nursery was the front-page lead story.

You may feel slightly uncomfortable about talking to journalists but they are a force for good in most instances, especially at a local level. If you are a celebrity, you will no doubt fear the presence of a *Sun* or *Mirror* journalist appearing on your doorstep, but those types of hacks are in the minority. The David vs Goliath story is something that local papers enjoy immensely, and it makes for great photos. You may recall that local newspaper editors love photos with lots of people in them, because it means sales. Everyone likes to see themselves in the paper, unless it's the courts section. The key is to be clear in your own mind what it is you are trying to achieve with your press coverage. What aspects do you need to accentuate to the journalist? Are you going to write a press release? Can you conjure any interesting photo opportunities, if asked to? When you have figured out your angle, give the newsroom a call and talk it through with them.

Localism

Regardless of your political persuasion, an exciting new way of thinking has begun to emerge, often referred to as localism. This simply means the transfer of powers from central government to local councils to make decision-makers more accountable to the community. It is wrapped up in a wider theme being pushed by the coalition, namely that of the 'Big Society', which is pledging to help charities, residents associations and other voluntary groups to deliver and run certain local services. The principle is that you know what is best for your area, certainly more so than a pen pusher in a government department.

The Big Society was formally announced via the publication of the Conservative Party's general election manifesto in April 2010, setting out to reframe the role of government and to engage people to contribute to the way society is run.

The plans include setting up a Big Society Bank and introducing a national citizen service for young people. These initiatives will aim to 'give communities more powers', 'transfer power from central to local government' and 'support co-ops, mutuals, charities and social enterprises'. For example, there has been the suggestion that remote country villages which are not well served by public transport could be given powers to run their own bus route, supported by the government.

These are quite radical proposals, not least because the last major British political leaders, Tony Blair and Margaret Thatcher, both largely centralised decision-making. The former introduced all sorts of league tables and targets to monitor the performance of schools and hospitals; the latter introduced 'rate-capping' to prevent overspend amongst local authorities. Localism is likely to impact on a whole host of everyday aspects of community life, from the planning system to organising street parties. Many will see this development as liberating, although as always there are critics of the idea.

They say that the inevitable cuts in public spending over the next few years will make delivering the Big Society much more difficult as public bodies and voluntary groups face substantial reductions in the money given to them by central government. They also say that localism relies on two things often absent from local villages and towns. Firstly, do most people have the requisite time on their hands and skills to create and run their own schools or to arrange a community event? The most advanced plans for creating a new school have been in wealthy areas such as Fulham and Wandsworth, thanks to the backing of celebrities such as the writer Toby Young. But what are the chances of success for a single mother who is living on a council estate in Nottingham, where the need for better schooling choices is much more urgent? The *Telegraph* journalist Mary Riddell went much further. She stated that 'the sink or swim society is upon us, and woe betide the poor, the frail, the old, the sick and the dependent'.

Secondly, do we trust parish councillors, for example, to take decisions on things which may have a profound impact on your area? They are often not wholly representative given that such a high proportion of people who take on such a role are over the age of retirement. Will they understand the needs of teenagers who want to create a skateboarding park if the plans to build it upset other residents?

Although many of the concerns raised by critics need be assuaged over time, localism is undoubtedly an opportunity for you to better influence decisions in your area. Don't like the school choices in your area? Then band together with other parents to start a new school. Don't like the lack of housing for first time buyers in your area? Then put pressure on your council to meet the identified need.

Local referendums are also a significant development. The

principle is that if you do not like the proposed increase in council tax, over the rate of inflation, then you (together with a suitable number of neighbours) can trigger a ballot to decide whether to accept or reject the proposed increase. Residents would be asked to choose between the proposed rise and a 'shadow budget', which the council must also prepare within the defined limit. A no vote would leave councils having to refund taxpayers or give a credit at the end of the tax year.

This forces councils to carefully examine their cost base in order to avoid an embarrassing contretemps in the first place.

The big culture change is that the British are used to things being centrally provided for them. Taxes are high but many people are reassured that key services such as health care are provided free at the point of use. Getting involved in the community sounds like a huge amount of effort, and the reaction of many people will be 'isn't this what I pay my taxes for?' It's similar to the way people complain about litter, yet would not dream of picking up a drinks can when they walk by it in the street. The thought process is that they pay council tax in order for someone else to do that. Yet the simple act of taking responsibility, and seizing the initiative, is good for you and good for society as a whole. Less rubbish on the streets means fewer council-employed cleaners, which in theory means lower taxes. It is a virtuous circle.

But taking a role in the community does not have to mean doling out soup to the homeless in the middle of the night (although that is obviously an honourable thing to do), but just something which takes a few minutes of your time. That may be simple things such as voting in local elections, attending a public meeting of the local police force, filling out a survey on the quality of public services, to name but a few tasks.

Localism and the Big Society are going to take time to become ingrained in the national psyche, but they are here to stay. Despite the criticisms, David Cameron is wholeheartedly behind the principle and even Labour is broadly signed up to a similar idea, the Movement for Change. Once the powers have been devolved, it is difficult to see any political party announcing they would take power back from the people.

Conclusion

Lean into it

Although you are now armed with all of this information and ready to use politicians to get what you want, you still need one vital ingredient to make it work: action. The easiest response to reading a 'how to' or self-help book is to put it down and forget about it. The excuses begin to roll out: it does not apply to me, it is a nice idea, but I don't have time, I don't have the skills, etc. But you are wrong, and if you finish reading the book with that view then I have failed in my argument. It's the oldest cliché but you really can achieve anything you want, where it is in your power to do so. Every one of us deals with difficult consumer situations every day and every one of us has elected politicians who (in theory) represent our interests. The fact that you do not make these two facts work for you is your problem, not theirs. In fact, as I have already explained, it is something they would prefer to remain the case. Inaction means passivity and passivity means that companies will continue to get the better of you, and developers and others in your community will also get their way.

The thing that really scares the life out of corporations and politicians is your decision to take them on and beat them at their own games. And as soon as you do it, you will feel empowered and happier with yourself. It is about reclaiming self-respect, and changing the system by not putting up with it. But any progress requires momentum. Sometimes you can defeat yourself by looking at the challenges which lies ahead and getting intimidated. Your imagination works overtime but if you visualise failure, then that is precisely what you will end up with. By learning and practising the techniques outlined in the book, and thinking positively, good things will start to happen. You will feel more of a participatory citizen, and you will find yourself asserting yourself in the right way, rather than always accepting the poor hand dealt by everyday life.

The best advice I ever received in this regard was simply to 'lean into it', which means just taking that first step towards your goal and creating your own momentum. It might simply be tracking down the telephone number for your MP, or the email address of the chief executive of the company you are battling with. It's a start, and it allows you to gather some pace in your journey of political self-empowerment.

I think it's a case of taking your campaigning one step at a time. The tips in this book should hopefully provide you with ideas of how to win smaller campaigns in your own life, whether as a consumer or more widely in the community. Once these skills have been developed, and once you feel more confident, you can then move on to the next stage, which might be standing for the local council or even taking up the government's offer to create a school or run a local youth project. Localism should bring benefits for you as you use the tips in this book. By making local people responsible for local decisions, you cannot be as easily fobbed off by a head teacher or councillor telling you that a decision is beyond his or her control. And trust me when I tell you that lobbying a district councillor is easier than a Secretary of State.

The government is hoping that the newly empowered local authorities will attract the very best people to stand and participate. I hope this happens. My guess is that people in society all want to lead and be able to influence local decisions. The challenge for the coalition government is trying to remedy the main problem, namely that people have been so disempowered for so long that they have lost the ability to think for themselves.

But do not keep this information to yourself. Once you learn the techniques, please feel free to get passionate about what you can do. Although I have always intended to turn my ideas into a book, I have equally been happy to help colleagues, friends and family in winning their own battles. In fact, it was the inspiration for this book. So good luck on your journey and please make sure you let me know how you get on. Sharing your experiences with others can only help to create the combined force needed to exact real and lasting change to the way we are treated by politicians and corporations.

The last word...

Fundamentally, I envisioned this book as a 'how to' guide about how to get what you want as a consumer and in your community. It may even help you get what you want from your partner and/or children (although I cannot promise that). If its contents all seemed straightforward and obvious, then that is good. This book was not intended for people who do what I do for a living.

I hope I have encouraged you to think more deeply about politicians, rejecting the obvious response of 'they are all the same'. That is not to say that I am without cynicism. You do not need to look through a great deal of chapter 1 to realise that. But my cynicism is at least based on personal experience of the political process rather than simply adopting views which others spout at me in the media. My cynicism is also balanced with a great deal of respect for the political process too.

The political world is a tough and bruising one, but possibly one of the most exciting and exhilarating industries you can be involved in. That is fundamentally because politics, and lobbying, is more about people and their inter-relationships, rather than policy and ideology. All the failings of our politicians are usually ones we have too – egotism, stubbornness, ambition. But we need to understand that politics has changed over the past twenty years and it is never going to return to what it once was.

The industry has become professionalised and intensely competitive. In the world of retail politics, all three parties have been forced to coalesce around the centre ground. The British public, increasingly turned off from the process, has also forgotten how to hold politicians to account. Yes, you will no doubt point me to the rise of pressure group politics to show I am wrong, but they have become equally professionalised. I am talking about individuals and communities taking control of their own responses to the decisions taken by both central and local government.

You can call it politics for the age of the Big Society if you wish. Just as we need to stop expecting 'someone else' to improve our communities and then being disappointed when the change does not happen, it is up to you to seize the day. Do not just moan and grumble about the way things are. Band together with others and start fighting back with the same methods they use against you.

And then there is the corporate world. What a disappointment that has been in recent times. Whether it is big scandals such as Enron or subprime mortgages, or just poor customer service in shops, we feel constantly let down. Unfortunately the response has been equally unimpressive. We just accept that big companies can offer shoddy services in return for our money and we are powerless to stop it. We have been conditioned to think like this over many years of grappling with the public sector.

But there is another way, as I have demonstrated. If I had not taken on companies and individuals over the years, a train service would have stopped, a post office closed, my car towed to a council depot, my family would have been without heat and hot water for weeks and it would have cost me hundreds of pounds in unfair charges. That is just one person, in the space of a few years. Imagine how many instances you could have succeeded in if only you had decided to stand up and fight rather than walk off and grumble.

What I hope this book has demonstrated is that you do not need time or money to get what you want from companies and from your community. You just need to be smart. It is not just Toby Young who has the capabilities to make the most of the new emphasis on localism; he is no more able than you to plan a campaign in the community. When the nagging voices begin in your head, ignore them, set aside five minutes and start taking action. It will be the most rewarding thing you will do this year.

Resources

If you've got this far you'll know how important it is to have a set of resources at your fingertips, be it the contact details for your MP or the telephone number of the water regulator. Here you'll find some key websites that will provide practical information and aid you in your quest to getting what you want.

Politicians
To find the name and contact details of your MP use
www.parliament.uk/mps-lords-and-offices/mps/

Your MEP can be found at
www.europarl.europa.eu/members/public/geoSearch.do?language=en

To find the name of your local councillor(s) see
http://local.direct.gov.uk/LDGRedirect/index.jsp?LGSL=358&LGIL=8

Be careful of its errors, but Wikipedia has a short profile of all MPs: www.wikipedia.org

An in-depth account of the *Daily Telegraph*'s investigation into MPs' expenses is available at
www.telegraph.co.uk/news/newstopics/mps-expenses/

Corporates

Consumer Focus is the most important consumer watchdog: www.consumerfocus.org.uk/

Citizens Advice Bureaus are being given greater powers by government: www.citizensadvice.org.uk/

If you live in Scotland, try www.cas.org.uk/

In Northern Ireland the most powerful body is the Consumer Council: www.consumercouncil.org.uk/

For water-related complaints try the Consumer Council for Water: http://www.ccwater.org.uk/

The water regulator is www.ofwat.gov.uk

The economic regulator for aviation is the Civil Aviation Authority: www.caa.co.uk

The regulator for energy is www.ofgem.gov.uk

Email addresses for many senior chief executives can be found at www.ceoemail.com

The main government department for consumers is the Department for Business, Innovation and Skills: www.bis.gov.uk

Lobbying

To find out more about lobbying try the following:

Association of Professional Political Consultants at: www.appc.org.uk/

Public Relations Consultants Association at:
www.prca.org.uk/

Chartered Institute of Public Relations at:
www.cipr.co.uk/

For an alternative view of the industry go to the Alliance for
Lobbying Transparency at
www.lobbyingtransparency.org/

To read more about the successful campaign on behalf of the
Gurkha veterans see www.gurkhajustice.org.uk/

Social networks
The best known social networking sites are:
Facebook: www.facebook.com
Twitter: www.twitter.com
LinkedIn: www.linkedin.com

Polling websites
Some of the top pollsters are:
Populus: www.populus.co.uk/
ICM: www.icmresearch.co.uk/
Ipsos MORI: www.ipsos-mori.com/
YouGov: www.yougov.co.uk/

General
An abundance of political videos and clips are featured on
www.youtube.com

To find out more about the Big Society try
http://thebigsociety.co.uk/

Details of the 2010 British Social Attitudes Survey can be
found at:
www.natcen.ac.uk/study/british-social-attitudes-26th-report

Author biography

Scott Colvin is an Associate Partner at Finsbury, one of the world's leading financial, regulatory and political communications agencies. Previously he was Head of Group Public Affairs at BAA Airports Ltd, the owners of Heathrow Airport.

Prior to his time at BAA, Scott was a senior consultant at a global communications firm, providing political advice to a range of FTSE-100 companies. Scott started his career as an adviser to Nigel Waterson MP, then the Conservative Party's shadow minister for local government. He then worked as a campaigns specialist at Conservative Central Office under three leaders: William Hague, Iain Duncan Smith and Michael Howard.

Between 2004 and 2008 Scott served as a councillor in Reigate and Banstead. He is married with two children and lives in Surrey.

Follow Scott on Twitter for useful tips and further information on campaigning and consumer issues: @scottcolvin

THE PRIME MINISTERS WHO NEVER WERE
A collection of political counterfactuals
Edited by Francis Beckett

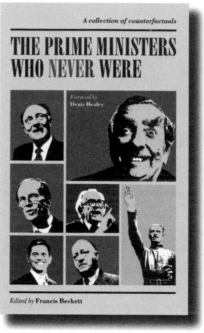

Back in the days of the smoke-filled rooms, the Tory grandee Lord Salisbury, who could not pronounce his Rs, invited the Cabinet into his room one by one and asked: 'It is Wab or Hawold?' The smart money was on them all saying Wab...

Had J. R. Clynes pipped Ramsay MacDonald to the party leadership, the millworker who'd left school at ten would have become Labour's first Prime Minister. In the dark days of war, Lord Halifax had first refusal on the premiership ahead of Winston Churchill. Both Hugh Gaitskell and John Smith would have been Prime Minister but for their sudden, early deaths.

Each of the chapters in this book of political counterfactuals describes a premiership that never happened, but might easily have done had the chips fallen slightly differently.

256pp hardback • £14.99 • Available now

www.bitebackpublishing.com

SO YOU WANT TO BE A
POLITICAL JOURNALIST

Edited by Sheila Gunn

While there is plenty of debate about the current state of politics and journalism, the aspiring political reporter receives little guidance. Do you understand the language of Westminster and Whitehall? Do unscrupulous spin doctors simply spoon-feed you stories? How far can you push your own political agenda? And just how do you get your big break?

With chapters on starting out in the trade, where to find the story and how to report it, and advice on dealing with the political classes, this book is the essential guide for journalism students, trainees and cub reporters working at every level of our political system. Edited by Sheila Gunn, former political reporter on *The Times* and spin doctor to John Major, *So You Want to Be a Political Journalist* features contributions from a wide range of current and former political journalists from print, broadcast and online media.

304pp paperback • £14.99 • Available now

www.bitebackpublishing.com

SPEAKING TO LEAD
How to make speeches that make a difference
John Shosky

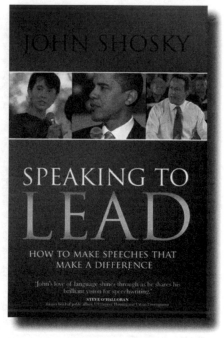

As a speechwriter and consultant, John Shosky's credentials are impeccable. During the last twenty-five years he has worked with people at the highest levels of government and business, including three presidential administrations and many top executives from Fortune 500 companies. In this book Shosky distils his incomparable know-how into an accessible practical guide to the essentials of his art.

Speaking to Lead teaches the importance and use of speech as action: a tool to fix problems and push issues forward. As the title suggests, from the boardroom to the podium, this is a book for leaders.

288pp paperback • £14.99 • Available now

www.bitebackpublishing.com

SO YOU WANT TO BE A POLITICIAN

Edited by Shane Greer

So You Want to be a Politician is a must read for any first time candidate or anyone looking to put together and run an effective campaign at any level of public life. This accessible, practical guide offers common-sense advice for almost any scenario.

Featuring contributions and advice from some of the leading names in contemporary British campaigning, *So You Want to be a Politician* is an essential resource that some of today's serving politicians could make good use of.

304pp paperback • £14.99 • Available now

www.bitebackpublishing.com